THRONE ROOM

Prayer

PRAYING WITH
JESUS ON THE
SEA OF GLASS

BRIAN & CANDICE SIMMONS

BroadStreet
PUBLISHING

BroadStreet Publishing® Group, LLC

Savage, Minnesota, USA

BroadStreetPublishing.com

Throne Room Prayer: Praying with Jesus on the Sea of Glass

Copyright © 2018 Brian and Candice Simmons

978-1-4245-5782-0 (softcover)

978-1-4245-5783-7 (e-book)

Unless indicated otherwise, all Scripture quotations are from The Passion Translation®. Copyright © 2017, 2018 by BroadStreet Publishing Group. thePassionTranslation.com. Used by permission. Scripture quotations marked NIV are taken from the Holy Bible, New International Version®, NIV® copyright ©1973, 1978, 1984, 2011 by Biblica, Inc.® Used by permission. All rights reserved worldwide.

Stock or custom editions of BroadStreet Publishing titles may be purchased in bulk for educational, business, ministry, fundraising, or sales promotional use. For information, please email info@broadstreetpublishing.com.

Cover and interior by GarborgDesign.com

Printed in the United States of America

18 19 20 21 22 5 4 3 2 1

CONTENTS

INTRODUCTION

Like most believers, I (Brian) have struggled through my prayer journey with typical highs and lows. There have been days that I really felt as though I could pray without stopping—it was a sheer joy to be with Jesus and to pour out my heart to Him! And on other days, well, not so much. In my journey, I'm learning to lean on my Beloved and become a prayer partner with Jesus in the heavenly realm. He has become my prayer life. These notes reflect this process of becoming one with Jesus in prayer.

Many people have made rich deposits in my life, deposits that have taught me about prayer. A dear brother was led by God in the first months of my new life in Christ to be a prayer partner with me. As a young believer, this made all the difference, for I felt so weak and inadequate. The memories I have of praying with Bob Bence are sweet indeed. Many could testify of the presence of the Lord that is released when Bob enters the room. He taught me that I could pray at any time, and for anything, with bold faith and with tears.

I also had older men that influenced me by living what they taught about prayer. Most of them are now in heaven enjoying their eternal reward: Duane Stous, Jim Ostewig, Robert Kaminsky, and Clarence Preedy. I am grateful for their impact and their challenge to me to become a man of prayer.

Yet there are three men who stand out to me as powerful examples of praying men. Their lives and their prayers have imprinted my life: Mike Bickle, a fervent man of God who has made prayer and fasting his lifestyle; James Goll, who has taken a leap into the deeper waters of intercession and learned the secrets of prayer power; and Lou Engle, a friend who has changed the world with his fiery intercession and passion for God. I am thankful that these three—Mike, James, and Lou—"come up for air" long enough to tell the rest of us what they are learning.

But even beyond these three, there is a woman who has helped and mentored me in this prayer journey, my treasure and darling wife, Candice. She is one of the deepest prophetic wells on earth today. I have seen in her a ceaseless spirit of prayer that both convicts and soothes my soul at the same time. She has followed me to the ends of the earth as a covenant partner in our forty-five (and counting) years of ministry. How could I even speak of my love for her? Candice has taught me that Jesus loves to hear us pray, and what a prayer partner she is to me! I'm so grateful that she has co-authored this book with me.

Expect incredible things to happen to you as you read through this book and become a prayer partner with Jesus on the Sea of Glass. What you're about to read is the expression of my heart in longing to be one with Jesus, not only on earth, but also in heaven. The heavenly realm is my focus, my eternal delight. I am praying for you as you read that you will get a "jump start" in your prayer journey. Whether you are a mature or new believer, this book is for you.

In the following pages, you will be taught the basics of prayer, intercession, and being one with Jesus in the heavenly realm. Jesus truly longs for you and me to become the echo of His heart, sharing eternal life with Him, and changing the world through our passionate prayers. Apply your heart to all that you read. Go deep. The more you give yourself to this study, the more you will receive. Perhaps a chapter or two may seem basic to you, but it is always good to ensure that our foundations of prayer are deep and strong. You might want to look at the chapter headings in the front of the book and see them as rungs on a ladder, a stairway meant to take you to the Sea of Glass. And after climbing this DNA-shaped ladder, you will be soaring into the heavens in an ecstatic experience of Throne Room Prayer, in union with the One you love.

We have asked God to make this the most encouraging book you have ever read on prayer. Wherever you are in your journey, I have prayed that you would find here a booster-rocket on each page that will shoot you right into the glory clouds of prayer. May you have a good ride and enjoy the view! Hope you don't mind high places! Start by praying this prayer with me:

Dear Lord Jesus, you know that I love you. You know that I want to be your prayer partner on the Sea of Glass. Teach me to pray as you taught your disciples. Take me into your realm and make me one with you as I pray. Help me when I don't feel like praying to remember how you prayed in the garden of Gethsemane. I give myself to you to be taught to pray. Change my life as I learn to make prayer my top priority and my joy. Give me the prayer assignments that you want me to have. I give myself to you. I call you my Beloved, my Friend, my Prayer Partner. Impart your grace into my life today. In Jesus' name. Amen.

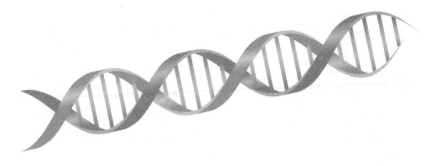

1

Thirsting for God

I long to drink of you O God,
drinking deeply from the streams of pleasure
flowing from your presence.
My longings overwhelm me for more of you!

PSALM 42:1

Join us on this journey to become one with Jesus on the Sea of Glass—to become His prayer partner. We'll talk more about the Sea of Glass in Chapter 22; for now, just know that it's a place of prayer that we learn about in the book of Revelation. Candice and I long to know Jesus, and we long to help others know Him. We want to teach others how to pray without feeling ashamed, guilty, unworthy, or inadequate. In reading through the Gospels, you'll never find Jesus making people ashamed about prayer or condemning them for not praying. He told His disciples, *"When* you pray"—not "Why don't you pray more?" We somehow sense that our Lord Jesus understands the battle we engage in as we develop a life of prayer.

Everything about you was made for God and created for His presence. And the true longing of your heart is to know Him because we were all formed in His very image. Just like every one of us longs to know our earthly fathers better, so there is a deep longing for all of mankind to know our heavenly Father. You might call it our soul-thirst for Him. When we enter His presence and come before Him, we are connecting with our True Source. It's in His presence that we're empowered. It's in His throne room that we come to life because there is absolutely nothing else on this side of heaven that can compare to communing with Him!

We're all created to be the Father's living vessels, filled with all that He is. He becomes our content, our substance—and we become His container—containers of the Christ! Without man, God has nowhere to put Himself, nowhere to pour out His very life. He can fill the universe with His wisdom and order, but He longs for a home, a place of rest. In a very real way, God needs you to become His completion, His fullness on the earth (Ephesians 1:17–23).

As we thirst for God, we connect with the desire of our eternal soul. Like a hunted deer panting for refreshment, we thirst for the living God. And this thirst can sometimes be overwhelming. As you go on this journey with us, you will begin to find that you just can't go on without a fresh infilling from the Fountain of Life, and prayer gives us that infilling.

After years of seeking Him, we have discovered that the way to live Christ is to breathe Him, and the way to breathe Him is to call on Him without ceasing. In 1 Timothy 6:12, Paul says, "Lay hold on the eternal life to which you were called." We've been called to eternal life. Now we must lay hold of this life by calling on the Lord night and day, day and night. By calling on Him, we breathe Him in.

The greatest lesson we have ever learned about prayer is this: Jesus is my prayer life! Jesus is our life, our strength, our victory, our hope of glory. He is the life and power of our prayers. Jesus in me is my prayer life and to be His partner in prayer must be the passion of every intercessor. His life in me is an ever-praying life! He ever lives to make intercession for me and in me! When you really believe this, your fear of not praying correctly will vanish! God has given us the privilege of taking hold of Him and borrowing His strength. Fellowship with the eternal God takes weak and unfit people and makes them His co-rulers, working together to bring His purposes to pass. You can become a walking prayer meeting on two legs as you intercede throughout the day. Busy moms, hurried men, students, and ministers alike can all mingle prayers with their daily work. An intercessor can maintain a spirit of constant prayer no matter what else is going on.

Calling on the Lord is one way that He draws us into His heart. He knows that His life-changing power is released when we spend time with Him. And He knows that adoration turns into transformation if we'll be patient. To love Him must be our supreme occupation. And the more we love Him, the more we spend time with Him, and the more we spend time with Him, the more our soul is transformed into His image (2 Corinthians 3:18; John 14:21). As we give Him our heart in prayer, He gives us His heart in exchange, transforming us from deep within. The more you give your heart to prayer, the more you'll experience His presence.

THINK OF THE HOLY OF HOLIES AS THE HEART OF THE FATHER

Think of the veil separating you from the Holy of Holies as being torn open by the Father's hand. Think of it as God's heart being torn open for you to peek inside. When you do, you'll see that He really is kind and merciful and forgiving after all. Prayer is the exquisite privilege of looking inside of God. He's not a condemning Father staring at you and wondering why it took you so long, but He is a Father whose heart has been torn open and is ready to receive you and hear your voice as you cry out to Him. He loves it! Prayer is not a burden, and it's not a duty. It's a privilege, and it's easy. It's a pleasure-filled experience of entering the ecstasy of His presence. When we understand the heart of the Father God torn open to receive us, we will run into His presence with delight and joy. Remember, prayer is easy when you love Him!

We pray not only to receive what we need but to know Him. All prayer is union with God. We join our heart, our spirit, and our longing with God's as we touch the eternal together. Our hearts are drawn toward heaven when we open our lips and call upon His name. Any need we have must be secondary to satisfying His Father-heart in prayer.

You are a priest coming to God with words, a priest with a ministry before the throne. Prayer is the greatest and noblest human action possible. Our true ministry is not what we do before others but who we are before the Lord (1 Peter 2:5–9). Most of us measure our ministries by their size, the number of people impacted, or books sold. But in heaven, our ministry is with God. We serve Him, we wait upon Him, we pour out our hearts to Him, and we listen to His voice. Yes, true ministry cannot be measured by any of earth's values; it can only be measured by heaven's glory.

Wherever you see miracles, you'll find prayer. God releases His power to work miracles in answer to the prayers of His people. You are one who can pray down the miracle power of heaven. We don't "hype it up"; we "pray it down." More prayer means more power. Without prayer, we can't do the works of Jesus, let alone the greater things He claimed we would do.

Miracles are waiting for your prayers. Everything we want is in heaven, and our prayers come alive in the heavenly realm. It's time for you to pray bolder prayers! Bolder prayer brings big miracles. Don't let everybody else see the miracles without you being included! If your prayers don't move your heart, then they won't move His heart! Pray with passion, and the miracles will flow (Luke 5:15–16; John 14:12–14).

Why Do We Pray?

The first thing that happens for many people when you mention prayer is a feeling of condemnation rather than a joy of communing with the Living Father. Many people think God is either mad or sad. They imagine that He's mad at every sinner, every backslider, and every Christian who blows it. Or they think that He's sad and melancholy over a world that's abandoned His ways. But we need to see that God is a happy God. He enjoys weak people, loves our prayers, and is touched by everything that affects us. And prayer touches His heart. Believe it or not, the Lord Jesus understands the difficulty we have in developing a life of prayer. He understands all our weaknesses!

Song of Songs 2:14 says, "How beautiful your eyes of worship and lovely your voice in prayer." Where is there condemnation in that? Guilt is the greatest hindrance to prayer. And guilt is such a poor motivator in the Christian life. It *will* produce results for a while, but it leaves a horrible aftertaste in our soul. You may start to feel that you never pray enough. And you may never feel as though you pray perfectly, with the right passion and the right words. But He's not keeping a record. In the ears of the Father there is a sweetness to our voice. "Come and pray to me," He says. "Let me hear your voice in prayer!"

This is an invitation for you to arise and pray. It is time to worship Him even in your place of need. If only you knew how sweet your voice is each time you call out to Him, it would bring you over and over into the secret chamber of His heart. Jesus calls to you: "How lovely you look there hidden in My love. Let Me hear your heart's cry, and I will answer you. Your voice is music to My ears—sweet, pleasing, and acceptable to Me."

He's waiting and longing to commune with you. It's time to invade His privacy. Rush into His presence like a child and love on Him. Let your words be free! Speak from your heart! And like any child would like to enjoy his own natural father, why not crawl up in His lap just for the sake of enjoying Him?

He is saying to the Shulamite, and He is saying to you and me: "Let Me take pleasure in you." Jesus always finds delight in His times of fellowship with you and me. Imagine Jesus looking at you where you are today and saying, "I enjoy you; I call you delightful; and I love you! Arise from your self-life and let Me break your shackles of introspection and fear that keep you distant from Me. Give Me your worship, for it is sweet." Just think: Jesus loves your voice in prayer.

Pray this today: Lord Jesus, you have won my heart. You tell me that my voice is sweet and that you delight to hear my prayer. Your love is the strength of my heart. Show me even more of your love today. I want my prayer to move your heart and to change me. Teach me how to value prayer as you did. Help me to rise early to seek your face and gaze upon your glory. I trust in you, my Lord and my God. Amen.

2

THE MYSTERY OF PRAYER

You answer our prayers with amazing wonders
and with awe-inspiring displays of power.
You are the righteous God who helps us like a father.
Everyone everywhere looks to you,
for you are the confidence of all the earth,
even to the farthest islands of the sea.

PSALM 65:5

Have you ever considered the mystery of prayer? It's both simple and profound at the same time. Prayer has changed the world and affected human history more than any of us could ever calculate. It's a divine, sacred, glorious mystery that will draw you into His heart. It's the privilege and the opportunity to lock arms with God and labor together with Him. It's life taken to its highest degree! It takes us into the timelessness of His presence as we speak with God and hear His heart.

Did you know there are over six hundred prayers in the Bible?

And that doesn't even count the 150 Psalms, which are prayers set to music. As we pray, we're actually partnering with Jesus and the Holy Spirit. Only a friend that truly loves you will always be there to hear your cry. Jesus is that friend: He will never leave or fail you. We cry out to Him because our heart is lovesick for the Son of God! We can learn of His kindness through prayer. He loves to hear our cry and loves to spend time with us.

We must be those who seek His presence, not just His presents. The Lord's Prayer begins with "Our Father," not "Our needs." Worship, not whining, is the highest form of prayer. As we pray, our friendship with the Beloved One deepens and sweetens as the true needs of our heart are answered by loving Him (Song of Songs 2:14).

PRAYER WAS THE PRIORITY OF JESUS

Many mornings, Jesus began with prayer in solitude. And Jesus was in prayer when the Holy Spirit came upon Him at His baptism. He received power, wisdom, and strategy by His intimate prayer life with the Father. We see Jesus praying over twenty-five times in the Gospels. During the last hours of His life, He prayed. On the cross, He prayed. Everything about His ministry was rooted in prayer. May we have the same longing for time alone with the Father that Jesus did.

> As he prayed, his face began to glow until it was a blinding glory streaming from him. His entire body was illuminated with a radiant glory. His brightness became so intense that it made his clothing blinding white, like multiple flashes of lightning. (Luke 9:29)

This was the "transfiguration" of Jesus found in three of the four Gospels. It is considered one of the highest moments of the life and ministry of Jesus. But what stands out to me are the words "As He prayed." It is *as we pray* that God is released within us to unveil who we are in His eyes. The real change we want can be found *as we pray*.

If it was a priority to the Holy Son of God to live continually in the presence of His Father, so must that be our priority. The very prayer habits of our Lord Jesus will be repeated on earth by those that seek Him above everything else. Jesus is the perfect prayer partner for you (Matthew 14:23; Mark 1:35; Luke 6:12).

PRAYER OPENS OUR SPIRITUAL EYES

God's Spirit can open blind eyes. We're all born blind because of sin, but when we are born again, God's Spirt opens those blind eyes. It's only by the Holy Spirit that we receive our spiritual eyes to see as we pray. And true spiritual insight comes with a humble desire to know Jesus. Many things will be shown to you as you pray. Expect your eyes to be opened to see into the spiritual realm all around you. For the kingdom of heaven is at hand and even close enough to reach. Sacred secrets will be shared with you as you make Jesus your lifetime prayer partner. Pray and God will open your eyes to see the glory of Christ (2 Kings 6:16–17; Ephesians 1:17–18; 1 Corinthians 2:9–10).

PRAYER IS A LOVE RESPONSE TO OTHERS

Every true prayer partner with Jesus will learn to carry the concerns of others. When we understand how powerful our prayers are, we will use them to pray for God's best to come to others. Prayer can lift the burdens of others, just as it lifts ours. When we pray for another person, we're participating in one of the most loving things we can do. As you grow in love, you'll grow in your prayer response to the burdens of your friends. Ask the Lord to show you today how to pray for others—and watch as miracles come to them (Philippians 1:7).

PRAYER ESCORTS GOD'S WILL TO THE EARTH

It is time to pray the power of God out of heaven onto the earth! The ministry of prayer is to bring the will of heaven here. We stand on God's side, wanting what God wants. It's as though our prayers paint a "bull's-eye" for the next place where God's power will fall. True prayer is discovering God's heart as we draw near to Him. And then as we join Him in intercession, we'll begin to see His will done on earth as it is in heaven. When you know what's happening in heaven, you can pray it done on earth (Amos 3:7).

True prayer is Christ in you praying through you to accomplish the Father's desires for the earth. It's true: Jesus Christ is your prayer partner, and He will pray through you as you pray through Him! It's by your prayers that God takes charge of things here on earth. The highest privilege of the church is to be the outlet of God's will. We escort God's purposes to the earth. We can pull down the future into the present with our prayers of faith (Matthew 6:10; Psalm119:126).

PRAYER BRINGS PEACE, COMFORT, AND JOY

Most of us are carrying burdens that must be given up and laid aside (Philippians 4:6–7). Prayer from the heart is like dialing 911. It is God's system for emergency response. Yes, He knows what you need before you even ask, but He wants you to ask. And when we do ask, we're turning our hearts to our true source of life, comfort, and peace. Nothing soothes the heart like prayer (James 5:13).

Just as a parent is stirred by the cry of their children, so Abba, our Father, is moved by your sigh. He is touched by the feeling of your weakness and understands you more than you realize (Hebrews 4:15–16). As we pour out our hearts before Him, we touch the flow of compassion in Abba Father's heart (Isaiah 30:19). Read Psalms 61–63 and underline the references to prayer and see the results of prayer!

PRAYER IS HOW WE RECEIVE WHAT WE NEED

What would you pray for today if you knew you could have it? Simply stated, we don't have what we need because we don't ask for it (James 4:2). Asking and receiving is the dynamic of prayer that relieves the pain of life and releases the substance of heaven. Whatever we need, whenever we need it, we simply ask the Father to give it. This cultivates your relationship as His child. Just as earthly fathers delight in caring for and providing for their children, so our heavenly Father knows what we have need of and will give it to us when we ask. Jesus once said to blind Bartimaeus, "What do you want me to do for you?" Jesus is still saying this to us every day. Do you have a need? Is there a burden on your heart? Is there something you want that only God can give you? Ask and watch Him answer! He's your Father and He loves you!

PRAYER IS HAVING THE PROPER FOCUS

True prayer must be addressed to our heavenly Father. There are about forty New Testament prayers recorded in the Scriptures; all are addressed to God the Father. We have no New Testament prayer directed at the devil. Jesus clearly taught us to pray to the Father (Matthew 18:19; Luke 11:2, 13). The prayer of Jesus in John 17 was directed to the Father. Even in the warfare epistle of

Ephesians, the apostle Paul prays to the "Father of Glory" (Ephesians 1:16–17). The prayer focus of the book of Revelation is to Him who sits on the throne or the Father and the Lamb or the Son (Revelation 4).

True prayer is focused on prayer from the throne room. If we pray from the throne room, our focus will help us to remain free from "preaching prayers." These are exhortations and descriptions of events rather than true petitions to God. Many corporate prayer meetings are stifled by "preaching prayers" that inform rather than the powerful prayers that exalt the Father, thanking Him and bringing our requests to Him on behalf of the people. Prayer must always be for an audience of One. Exhortation should not be done in prayer. The more we fill our hearts with the throne vision of Ezekiel 1, Revelation 4–5, and John 17, the better and more potent will be our times of prayer! When you pray from the throne room, you will pray from an "open heaven" mentality.

We become prophetically alert in the Holy Spirit when we pray from the perspective of being in the throne room instead of the prayer room. We won't be so concerned about who is praying, how they're praying, or how long they're praying. We're able to discern the "air currents" of the Holy Spirit and echo the heart of God through our prayers. For then the higher levels of His glorious presence are released through our united, focused prayer.

And true prayer maintains a positive focus. For faith to operate, we must pray with gratitude and confidence. Our times of prayer are spent praying for more of a release of the Holy Spirit, for righteousness to prevail, for grace to empower and mercy to triumph. It's more important to ask God for the impartation of good instead of having a negative focus on removing evil. Good overcomes evil. This focus enables us to pray in the love of God for those who are still trapped in darkness. It also provides "shock absorbers" for a prayer meeting when another intercessor prays differently than we do. Grace-centered prayers align with the throne of grace.

> Let the word of Christ live in you, flooding you with all wisdom. Apply the Scriptures as you teach and instruct one another with the Psalms, and with festive praises, and with prophetic songs given to you spontaneously by the Spirit. As the fountain of grace overflows within you, sing to God with all your hearts! (Colossians 3:16)

Paul prays for weak, immature churches and begins his prayers with thankfulness and gratitude for their budding virtues (1 Corinthians 1). Many of us do not even realize how negative our praying has become. To praise the Lord in the midst of our problems glorifies His name. As we pray with this positive focus, we'll free our hearts to carry the burdens of the Lord.

A sense of false humility will cause you always to dwell on what's wrong when the Lord commands us to rejoice as we come before eternity's throne. With a positive focus, we are enabled to hear from the Lord and dwell on His goodness, not the faults of one praying next to us. But if our eyes turn off of the Lord, we will invariably become critical of how others are praying, the words they use, the problems in their lives, and so on. Be thankful that they are entering in the best way that they know how. It's impossible to pray if criticism is in the midst of the prayer meeting. If we discern that something is wrong, turn it into prayer, not criticism. Let us be those who wear "grace glasses" and see one another with eyes washed with love (Song of Songs 5:12).

Pray this today: Lord Jesus, I find such comfort when I come before you. I step out of my pain and pressure and come to you, my precious Lord. My heart is at rest and quieted by your love. Help me absorb your glory, this atmosphere of heaven, and release it here on earth. I pray that my family will love you and know you as the God who answers prayer. I give you my heart today. Amen.

3

Beautiful Realms of Prayer

Pray passionately in the Spirit, as you constantly
intercede with every form of prayer at all times.
Pray the blessings of God upon all his believers.

Ephesians 6:18

The Lord loves diversity. That's why He made us all so different with different ways of viewing life. And because He made us all different, He has the wonderful ability to understand all of us when we pray with all our different needs. Some people pray with a prayer list of names and requests; some pray silently, others with shouting and declaring. There are as many different ways to pray as there are people on the earth. To try to press people into one prayer model is not wise.

Other than the Lord's Prayer, the Bible does not give us a preferred model of prayer. Rather, we find dozens of prayer models in the pages of Scripture. There are a hundred different ways that you come to God in prayer through the name and person of Jesus Christ. And there are many types of prayer in the Bible. Here are some of the basic categories of prayer:

PRAISE, ADORATION, AND THANKSGIVING

Praise is God's address. If you can't find God, praise Him. He'll show up! Try starting your encounter with God in prayer with extended seasons of praise. It's fine to be loud and rowdy; or you may choose to simply be quiet and reflective. Whatever your preferred method, it's time to praise the Lord! We have to learn the secret power of praise. It is not hype to praise God; it is the way into the realm of glory. Praise is like a pin code or password that allows you access into heaven. You leave behind the pressures of life and its disappointments, and you come gloriously into the heavenly realm—on the Sea of Glass!

Adoration is a form of intimate worship. Why don't you tell the Lord right now that you adore Him and look longingly at His beauty? Now close your eyes and speak it out: "Jesus, I adore you." Then thank Him all day long for what He means to you. It's that simple. This kind of prayer will free your heart from anxiety and care. As you become a thankful believer, peace will enter your heart (Philippians 4:6–7).

ASKING IN PRAYER

The simplest prayer of all is this: "Please, God, do this for me." Our God is a prayer-answering God. He'll not hesitate to answer the cry of those who love Him and ask in faith. Keep God busy answering your prayers. He won't mind. Let Him know what you need and be a holy reminder to the Lord. The more you ask, the more you'll receive. So keep on asking, keep on seeking, keep on knocking, and the door of answered prayer will be opened for you (Matthew 7:7–11). Go ahead, run into God's presence and invade the privacy of God! See yourself as a five-year-old that rushes into the Father's presence, oblivious of manners. Your Father can handle it. He's your Abba!

INTERCESSION

Intercession is asking God to intervene as you plead before God on behalf of others. It's the ministry of every believer. This is our highest calling. For we all have the priestly ministry of calling on the Father on behalf of others (1 Timothy 2:1–3). It's stretching our hearts out in love to cover others. Much of the remainder of this book will discuss the value and power of intercession to change the world.

DEVOTIONAL PRAYER

This category is your very own private time of heart-filling prayer. It's your alone time with Jesus, calling upon His name, meditating on His Word, and yielding your heart to Him. Watch as your inner being is built up and strengthened to defeat the enemy. During this time, try to incorporate all the different types of prayer: praise, adoration, thanksgiving, confession, asking, intercession, and warfare. As you pour out your heart to the Father, I promise you that your devotion will only grow stronger and your heart will come alive! Make sweet resolutions to love, follow, and obey Christ as you yield your spirit to Him. He will fill you with His presence. Remember, He says how lovely your voice is in prayer! "Every prayer of His godly lovers is pleasing to His heart" (Proverbs 15:8).

CORPORATE PRAYER

The family that prays together stays together. Corporate prayer is praying with others. It can be in your home as a family or in your prayer group. Or it can be in larger settings with hundreds or thousands present. Refreshing, enjoyable, life-giving prayer is coming to a church near you! To pray with others is more than valuable; it's crucial (Acts 2:42; 3:1). Every church and ministry must come together regularly for corporate prayer.

God will help you on this journey of prayer. You are connected as one Spirit with Jesus Christ (1 Corinthians 6:17), and He will help you, for you draw from His grace and from His life. The Holy Spirit has pledged to help us in prayer, giving us strength and passion as we lay out the pieces of our heart before Father God. There are many times that we would give up, but the Holy Spirit super-intercedes for us. Look at how Paul describes the prayer ministry of the Holy Spirit:

> The Holy Spirit takes hold of us in our human frailty to empower us in our weakness. For example, at times we don't even know how to pray, or know the best things to ask for. But the Holy Spirit rises up within us to super-intercede on our behalf, pleading to God with emotional sighs too deep for words. (Romans 8:26)

THE BASICS OF CONSISTENT PRAYER

SPEND TIME WITH GOD

The more time we spend with the Lord Jesus in prayer and in studying His Word, the more His presence will linger with us. It's kind of like when you're fellowshipping with other believers around the Lord. Sometimes it gets so good you wish you could just stay forever in that atmosphere with your friends. This is what true fellowship with God is like—it's lingering with Him. The Bible says that when we draw near to Him, He draws near to us (James 4:8).

Who wants to miss that opportunity of being near Him and dwelling in His presence? Not me! Remember Joshua. When Moses left the tabernacle, Joshua stayed behind and lingered (Exodus 33:11). This was undoubtedly where Joshua received His power to lead the nation of Israel and the power to win the battles that followed.

ASK WITH THE RIGHT MOTIVES

It doesn't make sense to pray with selfishness in our hearts, for the Lord sees our hearts and sees our motives. Love is the purest motive of the heart and should be the motivation that empowers every one of our prayers. As you fall hopelessly in love with Him, your goals will get lost in His and you will pray with the right motive (James 4:3; Isaiah 52:11; Psalm 37:4).

How could God give us things He knows would harm us? How could He answer prayers that will distract us from the perfect will of God? You may think something is God's will, but that doesn't make it so. Seek first the kingdom of God and all the things you ask for will be given to you. The kingdom of God is the place where God is King, His will is supreme, and He rules in perfect wisdom and will give us what we need (1 John 5:14–15; Matthew 6:33).

NEVER DOUBT THAT FATHER WILL ANSWER YOU

When asking the Father for something, it's totally silly even to ask for it if you don't really believe He'll do it. Why waste His time by playing religious games in prayer? Instead, ask Him boldly and in faith. Leave your doubts outside when you enter His sanctuary. He has limitless power to do what you're asking Him to do. Simply believe! Don't be double-minded with doubt in your heart. A single-minded devotion to God will give birth to genuine faith. Your Father is able to do all that you ask or think. It's time to believe for the unbelievable. Don't give up until the answer comes. (Luke 18:1; Isaiah 62:6–7; James 1:5–8; Ephesians 3:20).

RELEASE FORGIVENESS TO ALL

Jesus makes it clear that if we hold unforgiveness, He will withhold from us the things we desire in prayer (Matthew 6:9–15) Release forgiveness, and God will release answers to your prayers. You act the most like Jesus when you forgive like Jesus. True forgiveness is refusing to be angry again over the wrongs of another. Unforgiveness breaks your unfettered communication with God and locks you in the past. But forgiveness frees you in your prayer life and will release the Holy Spirit through your prayers.

Pray this today: Lord Jesus, I want you to become my prayer life. I want you to empower me and set me apart for you today. I come with all my heart before you on the Sea of Glass. I long to be one with you in prayer and to reflect your glory on the earth. I trust in you, and I trust the Holy Spirit to pray through me today. I will walk in the Spirit, and I will pray in the Spirit. My life will be your love offering today. I pray this in Jesus' name. Amen.

4

Hearing the Voice of God

*And the sheep recognize the voice of the true Shepherd, for he
calls his own by name and leads them out, for they belong to
him. And when he has brought out all his sheep, he walks ahead
of them and they will follow him, for they are familiar with his
voice. But they will run away from strangers and never follow
them because they know it's the voice of a stranger.*

JOHN 10:2–5

Prayer in its purest form is a love relationship with Father
God. It's an enjoyable relationship, not a religious activity. It's the privilege of soaring to the very throne room of
Father God to touch His face. Our souls are starved for this sense
of awe—to speak and to hear from the living God who loves us
and is waiting to share His heart with us.

Intimacy does not exist when our relationship is built on

one-way speeches. As I pray to God, I'm fully aware that both of us will speak and both of us will listen. As you practice two-way prayer, listening carefully and humbly, you'll hear Him speak. And this prophetic interchange is not just limited to verbal communication. You can also expect to encounter Him in various other ways. However you hear Him, this divine encounter will always do two things: it will change you, and it will give you ammunition for spiritual warfare. As you enter into prayer, the Father will not only speak to you, but He will also pray through you. You'll become one who hears from God in the secret place during your personal alone time with Him.

In the secret place, you'll discover His heart! This is the time and place where you'll be trusted with strategic prayer assignments. Instead of praying, "Speak, Lord, your servant is listening," we more often pray something similar to, "Listen, Lord, your servant is speaking!" Decide today that you'll take the time to wait on the Lord and listen for His voice.

It is imperative that your tools for ministry include a consistent life of hearing from Him as much as it is with speaking to Him (Isaiah 50:4–5). Ask Him for a listening ear. Marvelous revelations and a deeper understanding of Scripture await those who will ask for it. Linger in His presence and it will happen: you will hear His voice. Our Lord is known as the great "Revealer of mysteries" (Daniel 2:29, 47). And He will reveal so much more when you come to Him with a seeking heart.

Sometimes people ask me, "How do I know when it's God speaking and when it's the enemy? I don't want to be misled. I only want to listen to the Holy Spirit." Here are some simple guidelines for knowing God's voice and discerning when it's not Him, but the voice of the enemy.

THE DIFFERENCE BETWEEN THE SHEPHERD'S VOICE AND THE ENEMY'S

- Jesus is a gentle Shepherd, and His voice drips with mercy. Jesus does not condemn your personal worth; but satan[1] is a condemning and accusing intimidator.

- The Lord's voice is often quiet and deeply internal; satan's is intrusive and vulgar.

- The Holy Spirit calls and draws us; satan threatens, demands, and drives.

- The Lord's voice lines up with Scripture; the enemy speaks lies.

- The Lord's voice will bring a fresh "now" word that will change you and touch you; satan will lock you in the past.

- The Lord's voice is rooted in hope; satan brings negativity or despair that leaves you feeling hopeless.

- God's voice inspires us to love; satan inspires us to criticize others.

- Peace comes from God; satan brings anxiety.

- The voice of the Spirit will always glorify Jesus; satan glorifies self.

HOW DOES GOD SPEAK?

We all have a longing to hear God speak to us personally and would love to have Him speak to us audibly. We all want and need divine guidance for our lives—guidance that will teach us the

---

[1] Satan is one of the devil's titles or descriptors, so it is lowercased. It means "slanderer, accuser." Satan's actual name is Lucifer, which we capitalize as we would anyone else's name.

sacred mysteries of heaven and of His Word. Hearing Him speak seems too good to be true. You may be thinking, *Would the living God, the creator of all things actually speak with me?* The answer is clearly yes! But there is much we must learn about hearing His voice. We mistakenly think that He must speak a certain way, so we tend to box Him into our religious upbringing and narrow expectations. But when we become childlike in faith and simply listen, God will speak to us. But how is it that He speaks?

HE SPEAKS OUT OF OUR INTIMACY WITH HIM

Relationship leads to revelation. Intimacy imparts inspiration. It's as we seek His face that the direction, guidance, and wisdom come. Why would He want to shout at those He loves? God wants to have our focused, undivided attention so that the mere "look in His eyes" would be enough for us to know and understand His heart and His plans for us.

Lord, help us to be as close to you as we can. May we look into your eyes for all our needs knowing that everything will be met in you! (Psalm 27:4–8; 32:8–9).

HE SPEAKS ANY WAY HE CHOOSES

How does God speak? Any way He wants to! There are countless ways that God can speak to us. So often, we miss the voice of the Lord because we presume He can only speak a certain way. It's important to have an ear (heart) that will listen as one being taught. To be a true disciple, we must have an awakened heart, becoming teachable and responsive to what He says.

Your Beloved wants to expand your faith to hear Him through new expressions. Although many of the ways that He speaks are subjective and must be properly discerned, it's still worth the adventure to develop the "listening ear" (Job 33:14–26; Isaiah 50:4–5; Hebrews 1:1). We learn from the Bible that God has spoken in some of the following ways (please note that this is not an exhaustive list):

- Dreams
- Pictures in the mind
- Visions
- Parables
- Trances
- The Holy Spirit
- Angelic visitations
- The Scriptures
- Throne room encounters
- A voice speaking behind us
- Prophetic words
- Words in the night
- Prophetic actions
- Personal inner impressions/burdens
- Nature
- Signs, wonders, and miracles
- Everyday circumstances
- Animals speaking
- Face-to-face
- Through others

- Audible voice
- Still small voice
- Thundering words
- Riddles or "dark speech"
- Inner voice
- Conviction of sin
- His burning presence (bush of fire)
- Spontaneous ideas, thoughts
- A settled peace
- Closed doors/Open doors
- The counsel of friends
- Finances
- Unanswered prayer

Why not find a quiet spot today and open your heart wide to the Father? Ask Him to give you specific guidance for the decisions and dilemmas you face. Ask Him to give you ears as one being taught. Begin to praise and worship His name, the name of Jesus. Draw near to Him. Open your Bible to one of the Psalms and read it until it touches your heart. Wait in stillness … and then wait some more. Close your eyes. Let the Lord speak to you. And then when He speaks, make sure you write down what you hear or what you see. Then respond in humble obedience to whatever He shows you. Here are some passages that will help you begin your adventure: Psalm 81:13–14; Proverbs 1:23; Proverbs 6:20–23; Matthew 4:4; Acts 8:26, 29; 10:3; 18:9–10; Hebrews 3:15; Revelation 3:22; 19:10.

Pray this today: Lord, I'm ready to hear you speak. I'm ready to start this journey into hearing your voice and responding to what you say. I give you my heart and my ears. Speak each day as I seek your face. Help me to tune my heart to hear your whisper and to follow faithfully what you say to me. I am your willing servant—your lover—and I know you will speak to me. Give me a listening ear. In Jesus' name. Amen.

5

LISTENING PRAYER

Morning by morning he awakens my heart.
He opens my ears to hear his voice, to be trained to teach.
The Lord Yahweh has opened my ear, and I did not resist—
I did not rebel.

ISAIAH 50:4–5

It is so important to cultivate listening prayer—the heart that listens. We are quick to tell God our "shopping list" of requests, asking Him to break through and bring a miracle. That's wonderful! He wants us to come to Him and ask. But who will stop to listen to the Lord's heart as He will speak clearly in our throne room prayer encounters?

I always like to worship as a means to hear God's voice. The words of a song often become the very voice of the Father to our heart. It was that way for the early church. As they worshipped, God spoke to them (Acts 13:2). As you begin to cultivate a life of worshipping Him, it will all begin to make sense. It's not just about singing words. It's so much more than that. It's that place of allowing yourself to be vulnerable to the emotions of His heart as He touches yours. It's allowing the words and the melodies to bring you before Him and into His presence. Start worshipping at home, and as you do, you'll experience a softening of your heart to Him and He'll begin to speak to you! I can't begin to tell you how many times the Lord has ministered to me as I've poured myself out before Him in worship. It's out of this place of deepest intimacy that God will speak.

Lovers of God have been given eyes to see and ears to hear from God (Proverbs 20:12). God is the One who gives us the hearing ear and the seeing eye. God causes us to hear His glorious voice. When He opens our ears to hear, it is sweet beyond words. I have a friend who has been a pastor for many years who recently told me, "I can't believe what's happening to me. I never stopped praying long enough to listen to God's voice. Now, He is speaking to me every day!"

I believe it is possible to hear God's voice and His whisper every day. The key is having our ears opened by God. Are you ready to hear things that may challenge you or make you uncomfortable? God's voice shatters the "strongest of trees" (Psalm 29:5), so don't be surprised if it shatters your traditions and opinions wide open. To have our ears opened by God to listen is to be devoted to doing what He tells us to do.

Seven times Jesus stated that he spoke only what the Father taught him to say (John 7:16; 8:28, 47; 12:49; 14:10, 24; 17:8). Jesus' ears were opened to listen and obey the voice of His Father. Our ears must be pierced by this voice to make us disciples and teachers of truth. Hearing the voice of heaven is so important for you to enter into Throne Room Prayer.

GOD OFTEN SPEAKS IN PICTURES, NOT JUST WORDS

This is crucial to understand. God's language is parables, pictures, visions, and dreams. God doesn't just use words to communicate with us (1 Samuel 3:1–10; Amos 8:1–2). When Jesus taught the people, He always taught with parables (Matthew 13:34).

Interpreting pictures doesn't come overnight. It takes time to develop our understanding of even the fringes of His ways. Jesus' very own disciples didn't understand the things that He taught until later (John 16:29). Keep an open spirit to new ways of listening to His voice. It's so important to open the lens of our heart to receive. When you do, the Spirit of understanding will begin to shine in with the revelatory light that God longs to give us (Ephesians 1:15–18).

Because dreams and visions are so common among God's people, it's important to address them at this point. Part of the end time strategy of God is to pour out His Holy Spirit upon His sons and daughters. As a result, they will prophesy, have visions, and dream dreams (Acts 2:17). These dreams will reveal the wisdom and purposes of God not only for you, but for nations, churches, and individuals. Many of God's servants in the Bible were dreamers: Abraham, Jacob, Joseph, David, Daniel, Ezekiel, Joseph (the husband of Mary), John, and Paul. Even ungodly people received dreams that were from God: Pharaoh, Nebuchadnezzar, Herod, and others.

TRUST THE HOLY SPIRIT TO SPEAK TO YOU

The ability to hear what God is speaking comes directly through the supernatural revelation given to us by the Holy Spirit (1 Corinthians 2:9–10). You must learn to trust that what He's done for others He'll do for you! It's faith that opens our ears and keeps us alert to hear His voice (John 10:3). Believe that God will speak, wait to hear Him, and be ready to act. He'll give you your prayer assignments, and He may even cause a person's face or name to flash before you. This is God's way of alerting you to pray for them (Acts 9:10–14). Be ready for your faith to open your ears!

Whenever God speaks, it's always incredible! His words release such life and power. And because He's wise, He'll overlook what we want to hear to tell us what we need to hear instead. Give God all your "what ifs" and simply trust and obey. He's all-wise and all-loving. He doesn't have to explain everything He does or everything He tells us. We just need to humble our hearts and hear Him out. As we follow Him, eventually our understanding will catch up (Jeremiah 18:5–6). Never argue with the wisdom of God!

LISTEN FOR HIS VOICE THROUGH OTHERS

God has made us dependent upon others to grow in Christ. And He raises up Christian leaders to point us to Himself. We've been instructed to listen to them as they've been commissioned to care for our souls (Acts 8:30–31). And they've been placed in leadership to help interpret the ways of God. You'll find that, time after time, you'll hear the voice of God speaking the very thing you need to hear through them and others He sends your way. None of us are "know-it-alls" in God's kingdom. We need each other.

GOD SPEAKS THROUGH EVERYDAY CIRCUMSTANCES

Be careful not to over-spiritualize how God will speak. I once accidentally deleted an email I intended to send. Afterwards, I understood that my reply wouldn't have been God's heart for that person and was not filled with Jesus. God was trying to tell me not to send it, and I realized afterwards that God saved me from a lot of grief by that one seemingly accidental deletion. God will speak through the natural happenstance of our lives (Proverbs 1:20–22).

BENEFITS OF LISTENING TO GOD

Ponder this list of benefits that comes from listening to God. You might want to read them out loud more than once. Meditate on each one until your heart is stirred and begins to hear His whisper.

- Manifested sense of His nearness—Psalm 63:6–8
- Supernatural strength—Isaiah 40:31
- Direction and guidance—Isaiah 30:21
- Courage—Psalm 27:4
- Blessing—Isaiah 30:18
- Satisfaction—Psalm 63:5
- Wisdom—Psalm 90:12
- Prosperity—Joshua 1:8, Psalm 1:1–2
- Revelation to bless others—Isaiah 50:4

Candice and I love to discuss every morning the dreams we had the night before. For us, listening to God and doing what He says is the passion and goal of our lives. All we want to do is to have a hearing ear and tender heart to obey all that He says. Is that your heart's cry too? Imagine how your life can be changed by hearing His voice and following Him. Jesus did not say that His sheep *can* hear his voice, He said they *do* hear His voice and recognize that it is Him.

THE BASICS

1. *Keep your heart right with God.* Come into His presence clean and pure. You must leave all your bitterness and unforgiveness with Him. Then you can enter with the joy of the Lord in your heart (Psalm 66:18; Isaiah 59:1–2).

2. *Enter with a thankful heart.* Unrelenting gratitude for what God has done for you is the secret to a powerful prayer life. King David made many mistakes, but he praised God all the way through his personal "wilderness" until he got to the other side. Cultivate a grateful heart and come before Him with thanksgiving.

3. *Admit your weakness.* This is how we grow. God uses our weaknesses as a platform for His strength. It is OK in God's kingdom to be weak. The Lord loves to be our strength. He becomes for us our wisdom and our salvation (1 Corinthians 1:30). Scripture says that the weakest among us will be like David (Zechariah 12:8).

4. *Focus on God's power to meet your need.* Just believe that God is able to answer your cry and supply your every need (Philippians 4:19). That's faith!

5. *Let nothing keep you from giving yourself to prayer.* It's your lifeline to heaven. Be addicted! Be fervent! Become a walking house of prayer; prayer on two legs!

Pray this today: Lord Jesus, you are the kind and gentle Shepherd who leads your flock. You have promised me that your sheep will hear your voice—and I am one of your sheep. Speak to me, Lord, any way you want to. Cause my heart to know your voice and to hear all that you desire to speak to me. I will read your Word and apply it to my heart, listening daily for your voice to guide me. Thank you for every word that you speak to me, for your words are Truth and Life. Amen!

6

HEARING GOD'S VOICE

Surrender your anxiety!
Be silent and stop your striving
and you will see that that I am God.

PSALM 46:10

When God does speak to you, it'll be awesome and at times bewildering. One morning before the sun rose over the jungle, I (Brian) was up early praying and seeking the Lord. I quieted my heart and began to pray. Suddenly, I heard a voice. It was not inside me or simply in my mind. I *heard* a voice. God spoke in such a clear fashion to me that morning that I can only describe it as an audible voice that surrounded me. He spoke a message to me that changed the course of my life and the life of my precious family. This voice was clear and unmistakable, giving me guidance. One of the things He said to me that morning was that we were to leave our jungle village and return to North America. But a doubt lingered. *Is this really you, Lord?*

I walked into each room of our house to make sure no one was playing a trick on me. Candice was asleep, and in the other rooms, I saw our three children. All were fast asleep. My heart was thumping. As I sat back down with my open Bible, I said, "Lord, if this is really you, then say it again to me." The room filled with a silvery mist and the voice of the Lord repeated to me exactly the words I first heard. With my doubt removed, I waited for my wife to awaken so I could share with her the change in our plans. God is not mute, not hesitant to speak to His children who love Him.

Let God stretch your understanding, for His ways are not your ways. Be prepared for surprises! God's communication with us is Spirit to spirit. I have never heard that voice again like I did that early morning. Perhaps He will speak to me again like that, but perhaps not. I have learned to follow Him and let Him speak to me according to His timing and His plan.

TURN OFF YOUR PROBLEMS

To wait in silence before God is a lost art. As the presence of the Lord fills your heart, it's good to wait quietly for Him to speak. It's so important to take that time to be alone, in solitude with Him. He loves it! For centuries, God's people have found solitude and quietness as a doorway into His presence and into hearing His heart. One of the biggest secrets for receiving revelation is meditation (Proverbs 8:32–35). We are told throughout the Scriptures to meditate upon the Word of God (Psalm 1:2, Joshua 1:8). King David frequently meditated on the goodness of the Lord and would awake in God's presence (Psalm 139:17–18). Dedicate both evening and morning to hearing from Him (Psalm 119:147–148). Fresh revelation is yours for the asking. Meditate on Him in the evening and in the morning and wait and watch as manna descends from heaven.

A heart filled with anxiety and worry won't be able to hear God clearly. You need to lay aside whatever it is that's troubling you. Give it to God and know that He's in control (Philippians 4:6–7). If you're feeling troubled about something, pray. It's not a signal to worry! Our emotions are often no help at all. They may hinder us from hearing what God is trying to say. The best thing we can do is pray. Then not only will He relieve the burden, but He'll speak to us about our part. Prayer changes things! Worry never changes a thing.

And don't forget this: it is always right to ask God for confirmation from His Holy Word. He will not go against His Word, but I've found He's quite willing to go against my understanding of His Word. We not only need to lay aside our worries, we need to lay aside our traditions and opinions if we truly desire to hear His Voice. God will often speak through the pages of His inspired Word, so be quick to lay aside your limitations and come to God with an open Bible and a tender heart. Honor the Word of God, and the Lord will make sure you hear from Him!

The written Scriptures must have the final say in all our dreams, visions, and prophetic revelations. So often, our opinions of God's Word will keep us from correctly hearing the Word of the Lord. But the Lord will never contradict His Word, and He's not afraid to contradict our opinions and traditions regarding His Word. "Standing firm in the heavens and fastened to eternity is the Word of God" (Psalm 119:89).

WRITE IT IN A JOURNAL

Great treasures are found in even one word from the Lord. You may not understand what He's saying to you now, but you will later. Write it in a journal and watch God open your understanding over time! Many intercessors have found it very helpful to keep a prayer journal and to record any words that God gives them in prayer. God holds these words in high esteem, and so should we. It's so important that we write the revelation down so that we don't lose it (Habakkuk 2:2).

We're to wage war with the Word of God and the prophetic words that He gives us. Use the Word of God like Jesus did when He said to satan, "It is written!" (Matthew 4:4, 7, 10). However, don't forget to use the words God has given to you through prophecy, dreams, and visions as well. These words, when interpreted properly, also give you even more ammunition for your prayer life (Daniel 7:1).

Even the Lord's prophets in the Bible were often puzzled over what God said to them. Sometimes God will speak of something that will come later. We must be patient and wait for God to make it clear. He's always on time. One day with the Lord is like a thousand years. He doesn't live under the constraints of our schedules and ideas. God will always move in the fullness of time. Receiving revelation from God places us in a position of greater responsibility to walk in wisdom. When you don't understand, wait for it. For now, record it and save it for a later day (Habakkuk 2:3).

It's not wise to set time limits for God. Your faith may be tested! It's always best to wait on Him and let Him decide what's best for you. You're really blessed if you determine never to be offended by the way that He deals with you! People have missed incredible opportunities because they had limited the timing for God to move on their behalf. The Lord often waits until the eleventh hour to move in power (Romans 5:6).

THE HOLY SPIRIT

No one can ever take the place of the Holy Spirit. We must

tune our hearts to hear the Lord, not just those who speak for Him. As you go on into Christ-likeness, you must develop a heart that will seek the Lord for yourself. We must desire intimacy, not just information. Beware of living off others' faith instead of seeking God's heart for yourself (1 John 2:27).

As you begin this adventure of hearing God, there may be times when you may think that God has spoken to you only to learn later that you were listening to your own heart. Our inner thoughts may need realigning. Mature friends of God who esteem and have an understanding of what the will of the Lord is will distinguish between human impressions and God's voice. Some of the ways we think may need alignment with His. The Lord allows us to hear those thoughts so that He can help us adjust our thinking and show us our need to repent and be changed into His likeness.

A willing heart will be a hearing heart. Always do the last thing He gave you to do before you seek the next step. As you walk in the light you have, the Lord will give you more light (Psalm 36:9). When our will is yielded to God, you can expect the Holy Spirit to lead you even further. The Lord is patient to wait until our obedience is complete (Joshua 1:7).

However, it's not always wise to share your revelation with others. It is highly likely that they will not value what God is saying to you. Wisdom requires that we hold back from telling everything God gives us. Those who consistently hear from God will be quick to veil their knowledge in humility. Most of the time, when we blurt out what God is telling us, our motives are mixed with a desire to be seen by others as one who is closer to God than we truly are. Wait until God releases you to share your revelation with others. Paul the apostle waited fourteen years before he shared some of the experiences God had given him (2 Corinthians 12:1–10) while Joseph shared his and ended up in a pit (Genesis 37:5–23).

TRY ASKING GOD QUESTIONS

Have you ever thought of simply asking God a question before you go to bed at night? This is one way of receiving incredible wisdom and guidance from the Father. We must stay in constant communication with Him. Jesus said, *ask* and it shall be given (Matthew 7:7). He gave no condition or qualification to His statement. We can ask for anything and everything, including answers to questions about the Scripture, our future, decisions in our life, ministry direction—anything (Daniel 12:8; Psalm 16:7; 27:4; Jeremiah 33:3).

Why not ask God your questions before you sleep? If you've been saying God never speaks to you, here's a challenge. For the next seven nights, ask the Lord a specific question and trust Him to speak to you before you awake in the morning. In Daniel 2:29 and 47, God is called "the Revealer of Mysteries." Whatever you need, He has the answer. If you're lacking wisdom about something today, just ask Him and He'll give you the answer (James 1:5). Even Jesus, the greatest prayer example of all, asked questions to learn the wisdom of God (Luke 2:46–47). And the disciples were always asking questions of Him (Luke 11:1; Mark 7:17). Great and unsearchable things that you've never even dreamed are awaiting you as you ask.

Pray this today: Lord, I know you speak to me, but sometimes I don't listen. I choose today to hear your voice. Speak to me. Give me an open ear to hear your voice and grace to follow you. Amen.

7

PRIESTS OF THE PLANET!

So he is able to save fully from now throughout eternity,
everyone who comes to God through him,
because he lives to pray continually for them.

HEBREWS 7:25

How could we speak of prayer without taking a look at our example, our Magnificent Intercessor, Jesus? He is our mediator. Every one of us needs an intercessor: someone to come to God on our behalf (Job 9:32–33). God Himself saw that we had no one to intercede, so He supplied the need by sending us His Son! Prayer was and is the most important part of the present ministry of our risen Lord. Christ's ministry did not end with His death. When He was raised by resurrection power, He entered another ministry for us: the ministry of intercession. This prayer ministry of Jesus goes on even while you are reading this page because "He lives to pray continually for them" (Hebrews 7:25).

This One, who is fully man and fully God, is found before the Father in prayer for us. To find Jesus is to find Him praying. To really know the glorious Man, Christ Jesus, is to know an Intercessor. His full life and love are given over to prayer as He is surrounded by the Father's glory. More than anyone else, we love Him because He ever lives to intercede for us. Just think about it, our Lord Jesus is occupied with praying for you! This is His primary task as He dwells at the Father's right hand. He doesn't primarily live to judge, to demonstrate power, or to command angels. His special divine vocation is to intercede for His people.

Can you imagine what Jesus is asking the Father to do for you today? It's by His prayers that we've been saved from sin, self, and satan. Will you partner with Him, yield to God, and become an answer to the prayers of the Son of God? Jesus Christ wants to give you His voice in prayer. He invites you to join in His prayer time with the Father.

EVERY BELIEVER A PRIEST

Today, every believer is called a priest (Revelation 1:6; 1 Peter 2:5, 9). We are the priests of this planet. And all of us have the privilege of bringing the burdens of others before the Lord in prayer. We have become a "go-between," bringing the burdens of others to God. This type of prayer is called intercession. What a privilege we have! This is not for the few but for all. No one could say that this standard of prayer is too high or unattainable. As His priest, your true ministry is before the throne of God, not merely on earth before men. Likewise, every church is called to be an interceding church and must actively pursue this priestly ministry of intercession. It's part of our job description.

This means that you, a follower of Jesus Christ, are a priest of this planet! As Revelation 5:10 says, "You have chosen us to serve our God and formed us into a kingdom of priests who reign on the earth." From kings and priests flow power, influence, and blessing. In the king, power flows down; in the priest, power rises up and prevails with God. Jesus is the King-Priest, but He invites us into this ministry as His bride. We become heavenly Jacobs who prevail with God and become princes with power to move heaven.

By standing as a priest before God, I share the very glory of Jesus the God-Man. My true ministry is never what I am before men; instead, it's what I am before God. It's the work of a priest to worship and intercede before God. The Old Testament priest was one who represented the people before God. He was to carry the burdens of the people into the presence of the Lord. Over his heart, he carried the twelve tribes in the form of a special breastplate embedded with twelve precious stones. The apostle John wrote in Revelation 21 that he saw the Bridal City—the New Jerusalem—with these twelve jewels as gates or entryways. This was a picture of a miniature New Jerusalem being carried over the heart of the Priest as he ministered before God. The magnified breastplate becomes the New Jerusalem. In essence, the New Jerusalem is where God and man mingle as one.

The priests in Exodus 30 were given the responsibility of burning incense upon the altar at least twice daily—in the morning and in the evening. This activity was to be a perpetual ministry throughout all generations (Leviticus 6:13). We too, as new covenant priests, must be faithful to keep the fires of intercession burning continually upon the altar. It's never to go out! Fervent, continual intercession rises like incense before the Father's throne and moves His heart to respond to our cries. These prayers will fill up the golden bowls of incense in the presence of the Lamb (Revelation 5:8). As God's priests worship the Lamb in the beauty of His holiness, we'll be empowered to cry out day and night for God's glory to fall upon His people. Arise, O priests of God! Keep the fires of intercession burning!

The Lord has chosen to partner with us so that together we can enter the fulfillment of His purposes for heaven on earth. There's a longing in His heart to communicate this burden with His prayer partners, which we call intercessors. There are specific prayers that really need to be prayed, and He will give us the ammunition to pray them. But we must first hear His voice and understand His heart. Hearing His voice is so crucial for our prayers to be effective. We hear what's on the Father's heart and then pray what we've heard so that His will may be done on this earth as it is in heaven.

As you advance in prayer, you'll soon begin to discern other ways that God shares His burdens with you. Often, a strange heaviness will come upon you, and you'll sense that it's time to pray. You know that it's not the devil, nor is it a form of depression—in fact, there's never a time when it's not a good time to pray. It's the Lord's Spirit stirring you to seek His face and to discover what's on His heart! (Psalm 27:8). This is what it means to be His partner.

We willingly take upon our hearts the desire to pray until His burdens lift (Matthew 11:28–30). At other times, you may find yourself weeping for no known reason. Again, this is not depression or self-centeredness. The Lord allows us to feel the emotion that's associated with the problem so that we'll have empathy for the situation or person. And if you'll ask Him for specifics, you may hear more or have pictures flash before your mind that will provide you with more prayer ammunition and possibly something that you can do to put feet to your prayers (Acts 9:10–14).

The prophet Daniel took a prophetic word that was written by Jeremiah and prayed it through until an angel appeared (Daniel 9:2; Jeremiah 29:10). He knew the prophetic destiny for Israel was to be brought out of their Babylonian captivity and back into their land. Daniel didn't just read this prophecy and say, "Oh, that'll be nice." Instead, he interceded with all his heart. In Daniel 9:3 we read, "So I turned to the Lord God and pleaded with him in prayer and petition, in fasting, and in sackcloth and ashes." God's prophet stood in the gap between the helpless condition of his nation and the hope-filled promise of God. This is how we use every prophetic insight.

Remember the words of Samuel, "Speak Lord, for your servant is listening" (1 Samuel 3:10). Become one who waits daily at the Lord's doorposts, awaiting your prayer assignments and becoming His true prayer partner! God tells us, "If you wait at wisdom's doorway, longing to hear a word for every day, joy will break forth within you as you listen for what I'll say" (Proverbs 8:34).

INTERCESSORS OPEN THE GATES OF HEAVEN ON EARTH

As intercessors, we are given the very keys to the gates of heaven. We have the ability to stop hell's worst and release heaven's best. We have the authority to function in the domain of the Almighty (Matthew 16:19). We take our God-given keys and use them to unlock the heavens through the power of the Holy Spirit. And as "holy reminders," we act as God's secretaries, telling Him about the appointments He has agreed to keep!

Every promise of Scripture becomes a point of reminding God to keep His Word. And as we pray, the promises are answered. God lets us ask Him to do what He wants to do! May the Lord find a good secretary in you! This is the blessed mystery of being a prayer partner praying from the throne room with Jesus. It's not always large numbers of people praying but large prayers prayed by His people.

GETTING STARTED IN INTERCESSION

The Lord loves to hear your voice in prayer (Song of Songs 2:14–16). He calls it sweet and is touched every time He hears it. As far as He is concerned, you can't pray a "bad" prayer, for you are His precious child. His love filters out all our funny vocabulary and clumsy emotions to find our real heart. You can expect to find Him smiling, not frowning (James 1:5). He doesn't find fault in you when you come to Him (Song of Songs 4:7). Start in this place of sweetness and sacred confidence, and you will begin to see your prayer life grow as your capacity to know Him and His love grows. Those who are the most powerful in prayer are those who are ravished by His love. Let every encounter with Jesus in prayer be a precious and sacred time of sharing your heart with Him. Learn to listen as He answers and shares His most sacred secrets with you.

Pray this today: Lord Jesus, you have called me to pray with you on the Sea of Glass. I take my place as a priest before God making intercession for others. I love knowing that you are praying for me right now. I love to think of being one with you. Make my prayer the echo of your heart. Use my voice in prayer to move this planet closer to heaven. Help me to carry the concerns you have for the people around me and become an intercessor with you. I love you, Lord! Amen.

8

Intercessors Are Bridge-Builders

A man may be chastened on a bed of pain
with constant distress in his bones ... .
His soul draws near to the pit,
and his life to the messengers of death.
Yet if there is an angel [Hebrews "messenger"]
on his side as a mediator [Hebrews "intercessor"],
one out of a thousand, to tell a man what is right for him,
to be gracious to him and say [to God],
"Spare him from going down to the pit;
I have found a ransom for him [the blood of Jesus]"...
He prays to God and finds favor with him,
he sees God's face and shouts for joy;
he [the one on a bed of pain] is restored
by God to his righteous state.

JOB 33:19–26 NIV

Your prayers in the throne room build a bridge to bring others back to God as you stand in the gap—that distance between where the person/situation is and where God desires them to be. Between the need we see and the provision we long for, there is a gap that must be filled by an intercessor (a go-between). Every Christian is to battle in prayer for those around us in need (Ezekiel 22:30). It's time for us to become our brother's keeper by intercessory prayer that's motivated by love. We step into the breach for others, making our prayers a bridge for them to come to God. Now is the time for the church to arise with new anointing to build bridges for the lost and wandering ones to return to God.

Here are eight powerful truths we learn from Job 33:19–26:

1. Intercessors are like angels (messengers) to intervene on behalf of hurting people. When you pray for someone else, you become God's intercessor for them.

2. Intercessors have authority through prayer to heal even those chastened by God. Your prayer can lessen the pain and problems others go through.

3. A true intercessor is a mediator, a "go-between." You stand between a God who is ready to help and a hurting person who is wanting to be healed.

4. Intercessors are precious and rare; they are "one out of a thousand." God may be calling you into this precious and powerful ministry!

5. Intercessors can go to God based on the ransom

price of the blood. Jesus has paid it all, so we rest our prayers on the finished work of Jesus on the cross.

6. Intercessors find favor with God. You become like Christ when you become an intercessor. Others will note that you have been with Jesus in the place of prayer.

7. Intercessors pray until they see God's face (the answer to their prayers). Revelation always flows through intimacy, and prayer is the key to intimacy.

8. Intercession will restore fallen ones back to their righteous state. Nothing can be more meaningful in life than to restore a fallen soul.

INTERCESSION RELEASES OUR KINGLY ANOINTING

Earnest intercession makes every believer a king; investing him or her with authority so great that captives may be freed and prisoners released from darkness (Isaiah 61:1). This fervent intercession contains the power to transform and release people. We must persist in prayer with boldness, using the name of Jesus and the Word of God until satan gives up his prey. Our willingness to engage in this type of prayer will decide the eternal destiny of neighbors, friends, co-workers, family, and even nations. Whoever is not loosed from satan's grip in this lifetime will come under satan's dominion for eternity. Our prayers hold the potential for their release. Through our kingly anointing, our prayers have the power and authority to do anything our God can do!

The greatest thing you can do with God and for man is to pray.

God shapes the world through prayer. Our intercession paints a target on those who are in need of the gospel, and God then zeros in on their hearts. He sets His sight on them and strikes them with the arrows of conviction. What goes up will come down! Prayer is the key to turning hearts to God.

INTERCESSORS IDENTIFY WITH OTHERS

Intercession requires that we identify with the person and take upon ourselves the entire situation of the person that we're praying for. We may weep with those who weep and then rejoice with those who rejoice (Romans 12:15). When we carry another's burdens, we fulfill the law of Christ (Galatians 6:2).

Intercession cannot be made without paying some kind of sacrifice on behalf of another. Jesus paid the ultimate sacrifice for us and therefore has full authority to intercede on our behalf. Intercession and sacrifice are linked. The most powerful, effective intercession costs something. Your sacrifice of time and emotional energy will not be forgotten as you build a wall of protection or favor around those you intercede for. Jeremiah cried out for his people, "Arise, cry out in the night, as the watches of the night begin; pour out your heart like water in the presence of the Lord. Lift your hands to Him for the lives of your children who faint from hunger at the head of every street" (Lamentations 2:19). When the people are willing to pay a price in order to be heard, the heart of God is moved.

Paul was willing to be eternally condemned if it would mean the salvation of his race, Israel (Romans 9:3). This willingness and sacrifice of Paul gave his intercession power before the throne. Paul expressed the very heart of God for the people. When our intercession takes on that intensity, heaven will be moved on behalf of others. Both Moses and Paul were great intercessors who led God's people into the promised land of their inheritance. These warrior-watchmen carried great authority with God and ultimately transformed the lives of people (Exodus 32). This is what we need today!

INTERCESSORS ARE BOLD

It's time to move into the Promised Land of Intercession. Only the bold, the passionate, the pioneers need apply. Highly affective intercession involves boldness. Watch as the confidence of the authority of Jesus rises up in your spirit. Bold prayers will get answers. We'll change our prayer lives when we tap into bold praying (Hebrews 4:16). Those who understand they're one with Christ pray boldly. There are times for quiet brokenness before God, and there are times for bold interceding. The lives of others depend upon it!

Peter and John were bold when they prayed for the lame man at the Gate Beautiful. Their boldness offended the religious spirit of those nearby (Acts 4:13). Just like the spiritual boldness that brought a shaking with Peter and John, spiritual earthquakes will be released when the church learns to pray with boldness (Acts 4:29–31). Paul even asked others to pray for boldness to come upon him in his ministry of proclaiming Christ (Ephesians 6:18–21). Expect a greater boldness in prayer to surge into your spirit in coming days! God will take your intercession, as a prayer partner with Jesus, and change the world!

Bold, strategic breakers will push the lines back to where God has ordained them to be. Anointed forerunners of intercession are moving ahead and opening up territory right now. You can join them by taking on the burdens that the Father places upon your heart. Be bold and refuse to be intimidated by the enemy. Cast off all of his accusations and push aside all feelings of inferiority and condemnation as you intercede. This is the enemy's strategy to deflate you and cause you to be self-focused. Because of the blood of His Son, the Father has no memory of anything you've done wrong. As far as He's concerned you have no history—only a destiny. Three nails ended your history. Now you have only a destiny!

INTERCESSORS HAVE AUTHORITY

"I looked for a man (or a woman) among them who would build up the wall and stand before me in the gap on behalf of the land, so I would not have to destroy it, but I found none. So, I will pour out my wrath on them and consume them with my fiery anger, bringing down on their own heads all they have done," declares the Sovereign LORD. (Ezekiel 22:30–31 NIV)

God is searching for a man or woman. He only needs one person who will turn the tide of history. We come between God and His people pleading for mercy. This is good news! He's pleading for someone to come and persuade Him *not* to pour out His indignation! The Ancient of Days invites our intercession. This holy argument with God can avert or postpone judgment. Our intercession can be used to cut short, lessen, or delay righteous judgment until another day. The intercessor becomes one who stands in the gap between God's righteous judgments and the need of the people for mercy. Jeremiah, Jonah, Ezekiel, and the prophets were all intercessors who intervened on behalf of the guilty, sparing entire nations from coming judgment. God is earnestly searching for willing intercessors to come before Him to turn back

His hand of judgment and destruction. Intercessors must tap into the mercy of God!

INTERCESSORS BRING IN THE HARVEST WITH TRAVAIL

God wants birth in the church, not converts to our form of Christianity. As a mother travails in labor to give birth, so the church must travail in intercession for the nations to give birth to souls. With a holy stubbornness, we cannot let Him go until God blesses the nations with His great end-time harvest. The golden sickle of prayer will give the church the golden sickle with which to harvest. And the prayers of the saints will release "reaping angels" throughout the earth (Revelation 14:15–16).

The Hebrew word for intercession is *paga* which means *to struggle by prayer, to press forward, to travail, to weep, to come between, to touch, to reach, to strike the mark, to attack, to fall upon.* The Scriptures paint a picture of a type of prayer that is messy! You cannot have birth without travail. Every woman who has given birth to a child knows what travail is. The baby does not birth itself. The Hebrew word for travail is *yalad*, which means *the time of delivery* or *intense labor pain.* For spiritual children to be born, some intercessor somewhere has travailed and prevailed! When the spirit of travail for the lost is upon you, nothing else matters. You must labor until birth comes. And what grips God's heart begins to grip yours. It is almost like God is preparing an opening for the baby to come forth and travail creates that opening for new life.

Our intercessory travail is rooted in the confidence that God is love and wants the best for every human being. Therefore, we must pray to move God's heart, appealing to His heart of love for humanity. And instead of wrestling *with* each other, we must wrestle *for* each other in prayer. The backslidden will return when love moves us to pray. As we really begin to feel the heart of God for the end-time harvest, you may see tears flowing freely. The language of compassionate weeping never fails to touch the heart. Men can resist your words, but they cannot resist your tears. Jeremiah was known as the weeping prophet for the many tears he cried over the stubbornness of God's people (Jeremiah 9:1; Lamentations 2:11, 18–19). Paul was also one who daily warned the flock of God "night and day with tears" (Acts 20:31). And we learn this in the Psalms: "Those who sow their tears as seeds will reap a harvest with joyful shouts of glee. They may weep as they go out carrying their seed to sow, but they will return with joyful laughter and shouting with gladness as they bring back armloads of blessing and a harvest overflowing!" (Psalm 126:5–6).

Pray this today: Lord Jesus, I love you and want to be your constant companion. I long to be continually in prayer throughout my day. I want to cultivate a beautiful intimacy with you. Help me in my weakness, and give me grace to grow in my ministry of prayer. I surrender my soul to you! Amen.

9

THE PRAYER OF UNITY

How truly wonderful and delightful
to see brothers and sisters living together in sweet unity!
It's as precious as the sacred scented oil
flowing from the head of the high priest Aaron,
dripping down upon his beard and running all the way down
to the hem of his priestly robes.
This heavenly harmony can be compared to the dew
dripping down from the skies upon Mount Hermon,
refreshing the mountain slopes of Israel.
For from this realm of sweet harmony
God will release his eternal blessing, the promise of life forever!

PSALM 133

There's something powerful that happens when believers come together to pray. As we join our hearts with others at the "throne of grace" (Hebrews 4:16) we can expect an even greater impact. Prayer is meant to be more than just our own private devotional time with God. It's meant to be a shared experience with others in a corporate setting as well. The Lord loves to see His kids praying together with passion and with unity. You and I are called to be His prayer pioneers.

The early disciples continually gathered together for prayer (Acts 2:42). Corporate intercession was the consistent practice of the early church, providing the fuel for revival and miracles. Every church that is pursuing the heart of God needs to establish regular, corporate times of intercession. These united prayer gatherings will one day become twenty-four-hour prayer centers for every region of the earth as God re-establishes the Tabernacle of David among the nations. Listen to what the Father says about His end-time intercessors: "'I will welcome them into my holy mountain and make them joyful in my house of prayer. I will accept every sacrifice and offering that they place on my altar, for my house of worship will be known as a house of prayer for all people'" (Isaiah 56:7).

The Lord longs to bring joy into His house of prayer. Enjoyable prayer is even now being released into prayer rooms across the earth! For His promise is that He will give those who are dedicated to prayer great joy. And His love-sick worshippers are already filling the Houses of Prayer and finding prayer enjoyable as they spend time with Him.

HEAVEN WAITS FOR EARTH!

The movement of God must come to the earth by aggressive, even furious prayer. The move in heaven is controlled by the move on earth. Listen to what Jesus has taught us: "'Whatever you bind on earth will be bound in heaven, and whatever you loose on earth will be loosed in heaven'" (Matthew 18:18 NIV). This is in the context of united, believing prayer. There must be a move on earth before there is a move in heaven. We are given the keys and must utilize them before heaven will move! It's not heaven that binds first or looses first; it's earth. Our prayers must bind everything that's contrary to heaven and loose everything that God wants to be done on earth. The Sovereign Lord wants the church to control heaven!

Are you getting it yet? There's a power that God puts under the control of His interceding people. Just as Moses' uplifted hand controlled the outcome of the battle (Exodus 17:9–11), so intercessors are those who lift up their hands on earth and see heaven's grace pour out on earth's battlefields. Truly, God wants us to win and taste victory, but if we don't pray aggressively, battles may be lost. God will actually yield to our plea! The Father lets His sons "pin Him to the mat," so to speak, by intercession. "This is what the Sovereign LORD says: 'Once again I will yield to the plea of the house of Israel and do this for them'" (Ezekiel 36:37 NIV).

UNITED PRAYER: THE POWER OF GOD

Jesus taught His disciples that the power of prayer is multiplied when believers come together to intercede. One can chase a thousand and two can chase ten thousand! Using the mathematics of heaven, only seven praying in one accord could chase one billion! World-changing prayer will result when we agree with others and pray in unity. This is why Jesus always sent out His disciples two by two. To pray together in one spirit and with one heart is to touch heaven. There is a corporate model of prayer in the Bible that is not individualistic. We experience the blessing of heaven talked about in Psalm 133 when we come together in true unity. Jesus' words to us in the New Testament make this clear:

> "Again, I give you an eternal truth: If two of you agree to ask God for something in a symphony of prayer, my heavenly Father will do it for you. For wherever two or three

come together in honor of my name, I am right there with
them!" (Matthew 18:19–20)

Since we have this confidence, we can also have great
boldness before him, for if we present any request agree-
able to his will, he will hear us. And if we know that he
hears us in whatever we ask, we also know that we have
obtained the requests we ask of him. (1 John 5:14–15)

Throughout the book of Acts, we see the church actively entering into the power of agreement and coming together for prayer.
Our authority increases when the church prays in unity:

All of them were united in one prayer, gripped with passion, interceding night and day. (Acts 1:14)

On the day Pentecost was fulfilled all the disciples were
gathered in one place (praying). (Acts 2:1)

Then suddenly at that moment the earth began to shake
beneath them, causing the building they were in to tremble! And each one of them was filled with the Holy Spirit,
and they began to proclaim the Word of God with an
unrestrained boldness! All the believers were one in mind
and heart. Selfishness was not a part of their community,
for they shared everything they had with one another.
(Acts 4:31–32)

The longing of Jesus was that all His followers would be one in
spirit and in glory with Himself. There is a sense in which every
time we come together as one to intercede, we are bringing delight
to the heart of the Lord Jesus and, in part, answering this prayer.

Corporate prayer meetings are a kind of practice for heaven's glory—you will even feel heaven's glory filling the room!

Praying together releases heaven on earth and takes us into our destiny. There is a measure of God's Spirit that will not be given to the church until we come together in united, sustained prayer. He's waiting on us to agree with heaven! True prayer brings a joy and gladness into the prayer meeting. The Lord has said He would "make them joyful in My house of prayer" (Isaiah 56:7).

It's a religious spirit that wants to make every prayer meeting into a time of confession and repentance. But introspection, apart from the genuine conviction of the Holy Spirit, moves us away from God's heart, not closer. Yes, there are times to weep. As Scripture says, "There's a time to weep and a time to laugh" (Ecclesiastes 3:4 NIV). But when you have the bridegroom with you, it's time for joy! As our Friend and Bridegroom, we encounter Him with love and joy. Divine romance needs to be brought into the prayer meeting! We're His bride, and we earnestly love Him. How can we be negative when our thoughts are filled with the Bridegroom and His exquisite love for us? The Lord really wants us to enjoy our prayer time with Him.

There is such an interesting dynamic that takes place in the corporate setting. As we come together and place our full focus on God, we can engage our spirits at the deepest level. Our attention span tends to lengthen. Most of us can pray longer when we're together and the Spirit of God is moving in the room through one another.

Two are better than one: they can chase ten thousand distractions away. When hundreds or even thousands gather for intercession, power is released. And then we are enabled to engage with God aggressively rather than passively disengage while others are praying. It's almost like a healthy, holy peer pressure for all of us to stay united in the spirit. Those weak in prayer are taught, and those that are strong in prayer are able to lead and encourage without undue coaxing. And the icing on the cake is that the commanded blessing of Psalm 133 is released as our voices and hearts have come together as one. Something special happens when the church prays!

Intercessory prayer meetings are the womb of the church, birthing God's purpose. Many churches don't understand this and want to silence the groans of labor pains. But this is the type of travail that brings in the harvest. You may want to instruct those that are new to intercessory prayer about what's happening, but beware that you don't mistake true intercessory travail with those who simply make noise to have their own emotional brokenness filled.

The hope of the world is that an intercessory army will rise and take her place as the warring bride armed with the mighty weapons of the promises of God (Ephesians 5–6). When Zion travails, she brings forth her children! At times, it's best to wait and see what God is doing before shutting someone down from expressing themselves in ways that you're not used to … you may be in the midst of pre-revival travail!

Pray this today: Lord Jesus, I feel a deeper call from the throne room to enter into prayer with you. Prayer is where it's at, and I want to be on the front lines of your advancing kingdom. Make me a walking prayer meeting. Cause my heart to burn with deeper longings to be your prayer partner. I want to learn all that you have to teach me. Amen.

10

THE LORD'S PRAYER

One day as Jesus was in prayer, one of his disciples came over to him as he finished and said, "Would you teach us a model prayer that we can pray, just like John did for his disciples?"

LUKE 11:1

The prayers of Jesus were so powerful that His disciples pleaded with Him to teach them His secret. Jesus is our ultimate authority on and teacher about prayer. There are two things that we notice right away: effective prayer can be learned, and the most effective environment for learning about prayer is in the context of discipleship (a mentoring relationship). Jesus taught His disciples and continues to teach His followers by example. Do you want to learn to pray? Desire is the first step. Just say to the Lord, "Lord, teach me to pray!"

Students of the Bible throughout the ages have concluded that one of the greatest prayer models of all time has been given to us by our Lord Jesus in what is known as the "Lord's Prayer" (Matthew

6:9–13). In just ninety-one words in the English translation, Jesus models for us how we are to pray. When we were just children, we would go to church and recite this prayer in unison every Sunday morning. And now we can recite it from memory. For years after we experienced new birth, we rarely used this model, feeling it had been overdone. But now we recognize that it contains the wisdom of Christ that can be utilized in our corporate and devotional prayer times. Within the Lord's Prayer are all the elements of our devotional life in God and a progression of moving into the Holy of Holies. Notice the scope of this prayer:

- Worship—"Our Father, dwelling in the heavenly realms, may the glory of your name be the center on which our lives turn."

- Intercession—"Manifest your kingdom realm and cause your every purpose to be fulfilled on earth."

- Personal Petition—"We acknowledge you as our Provider of all we need each day."

- Confession—"Forgive us the wrongs we have done."

- Forgiveness of Others—"As we ourselves release forgiveness to those who have wronged us."

- Guidance—"Rescue us every time we face tribulation."

- Warfare—"And set us free from evil."

- Bold Declaration—"For you are the King who rules with power and glory forever. Amen."

Many today find comfort in praying the "Lord's Prayer" as it is written because it is indeed the model prayer. However, the Lord's Prayer also serves as a proven pattern to be used as a springboard to launch us into intercession. It's a wonderful biblical outline for corporate prayer. If you're having intercessory prayer meetings that are stuck in a rut, then try praying this model. Notice it begins and ends with a focus on praise for God and His glory:

"PRAY THEN LIKE THIS: OUR FATHER ..."

Our confidence in prayer is established upon our security and the love coming from Father God. We rejoice in the privileges of being His beloved ones, His favorite ones in all the earth. It's our great privilege and joy to call Him Father. The Father's love and acceptance is always real, even when we don't feel it. And it's always a great joy to approach Him in fellowship with others; He is our Father. And as children of the Most-High God, we have corporate privilege as our birthright. We are the "church of the Firstborn" (Hebrews 12:23) and therefore have the rights of a first-born. We step into our full inheritance as His firstborn sons and daughters as we call out to Him, our Abba, Father.

This is what it means to have God as our Father:

I am the center of His attention.

I am the subject of His concern.

I am the recipient of His glory.

I am the focus of His planning.

I am the object of His love.

I am His total and continual occupation.

God is *our* Father. He has family of many sons and daughters. As an intercessor, you need to pray in agreement or harmony with others. If we're in strife with others in the body of Christ, our prayers will be ineffective and without punch. Learn to pray in agreement with other intercessors before tackling difficult spiritual issues (Matthew 18:19–20; Acts 2:1).

Jesus sent His disciples out two by two. They were sent out with the power and authority to cast out demons and plunder the kingdom of darkness. Having agreement with others in unified prayer is a vital weapon for spiritual warfare. When we're alone, we become an easy target. If we have an independent spirit, which is a rebellious spirit, we're powerless to face our foes. Praying in agreement with others keeps us from deception and protects us from an assault.

"Dwelling in the Heavenly Realms"

To be enthroned with Jesus is our heavenly calling (Philippians 3:14; Colossians 3:1–3). Every time we pray, our desires and longings must turn to the dwelling place of the Lord. We find our heart's true home in the place of prayer. Notice the heavenly gaze of David:

> Here's the one thing I crave from God,
> the one thing I seek above all else:
> I want the privilege of living with him every moment in
> his house,
> finding the sweet loveliness of his face,
> filled with awe, delighting in his glory and grace.
> I want to live my life so close to him
> that he takes pleasure in my every prayer. (Psalm 27:4)

This heavenly attraction must fill our heart in prayer, delivering us from the need to be heard by men. Our cares vanish as we turn our thoughts to the One who is in the "heavenly realms."

"MAY THE GLORY OF YOUR NAME BE THE CENTER FROM WHICH OUR LIVES TURN"

We are to adore and worship His name! And everything we do must center on Him, especially our prayer. His name/names reflect His flawless character. As we recognize His name, we recognize His virtues and His beauty, causing us to worship Him. Too often, we come to pray and meditate on us, on ourselves. It's time to make the name of Jesus our meditation. It's a delight to speak of His beauty in prayer for His name reflects Him and His glory. All the names of God reveal what He's promised to be in us. Take any one of His many names and make them your mediation. Worship is the true way of hallowing (adoring) the name of Father God.

"MANIFEST YOUR KINGDOM REALM"

"Come, kingdom of God" is the cry of God's people in intercession. With a willing spirit to lay everything aside and say yes to this kingdom is a desire to say yes to change. We long to be under the lordship of Jesus, our King. We pray not only that His kingdom come, but we pray for our hearts to be conformed into His image as we subject ourselves afresh to His kingdom rule in us as well as in the rest of the earth. We say to our King, "Reign over me and all that is around me. I accept your rule and will obey you." When we gather for corporate intercession, it's good to pray that His kingdom come to our hearts, our homes, our churches, and to the nations of the earth. May we all lift up one voice as we pray, "Manifest your kingdom realm."

"AND CAUSE YOUR EVERY PURPOSE TO BE FULFILLED"

This is the longing of our hearts: to do the will of God and to see His purpose fulfilled in us. It's important to speak to your needs and say, "Be fulfilled, purpose of God! Be done in my family, my church, and my workplace." Proclaim the right of God to enforce His will over you and over every spiritual foe you face. This is a declaration of God's sovereign power to do within us all He longs to do. We were made for His pleasure, not for sin, discouragement, and fear. This prayer is also a prophecy that God will win your battles and release His wisdom to maintain victory in all situations. As you release these words in prayer, watch as it comes to pass. Take authority with these words: "Cause your every purpose to be fulfilled."

"On Earth"

Whatever God has in heaven, you can ask for on earth. Holiness, peace, victory, joy, worship, divine revelation, power, glory, freedom, and serenity … all of these virtues are filling heaven even as you read this page. Intercession pulls down heaven to the earth. Praying warriors will storm the citadel of heaven as violent ones who won't take no for an answer. We'll ascend the hill of the Lord with holy hands raised to Him, asking for the heavenly glory to come to earth! There are things you will never experience in God if you don't ask Him. Begin to pray that heaven will touch your earth, for you're made from the dust of the earth! This is your inheritance in Christ, and it's waiting to be claimed in prayer. Heaven releases itself on earth when the church comes together to intercede and ask.

The standard of the church must be a heavenly one, not a cultural one. We don't need the ways of men, for the ways of God are higher than man's ways. We can't rest, nor can we give Him rest until what's done in heaven is done on earth. We want heaven's worship, heaven's peace, and heaven's power in the church. May there be night and day intercession before the throne of God pleading for God to move "on earth as it is in heaven!"

"WE ACKNOWLEDGE YOU AS THE PROVIDER OF ALL WE NEED EACH DAY"

He daily provides all that we need. This is our promise in Christ. And we need to be praying daily for our heavenly portion of spiritual and natural bread as our supply. This is an incentive to pray the promises of God regularly. Take His promises and speak His "Amen" over all He has told you He would do. They're all to be fulfilled as we claim them and touch them in prayer. He provides both the material provisions and the spiritual "bread" that nurtures our life in God: fresh revelation knowledge, healing (which is the children's bread—see Matthew 15:22–28), and power for ministry, gifting, and anointing. These are all needs that you can ask the Father for in your daily prayer and corporate intercession and expect to receive.

Pray this today: Our Father, dwelling in the heavenly realm, may the glory of your name be the center from which our lives turn. Manifest your kingdom realm, and cause your every purpose to be fulfilled on earth, just like it is in heaven. I acknowledge you as the Provider of all that I need each day. I love you, Father-God. Amen.

11

The Lord's Prayer— Forgiveness and Freedom

Forgive us the wrong we have done.

Luke 11:4

We don't live very long before we realize the importance of forgiveness. We learn to live for God through the path of forgiveness. We've been made holy by the blood of the Lamb, but our "condition" doesn't always match up with our "position." As we live out our daily lives before Him, we need our confession (our walk with Christ) to line up with the one we're created to look like: Jesus Christ, the pure and holy one. For Christ is our righteousness.

We're like Peter, when he asked Jesus to wash his whole body at the last supper. Jesus told him that he only needed his feet washed. That's the same for us. As we live out our lives before the Father and walk through this world, we don't need our whole body washed, but we do need our feet washed again. Our walk must be aligned with our calling.

To refuse to forgive those who have injured or offended us is to keep our heart at a distance from the throne room. To come into the throne room is to come clean, drawing near with a clean heart. To be hurt is to be human. There is nothing evil with you being hurt by the words or actions of others. You can't repent of being human with intricate, legitimate feelings. However, our hurt feelings and brokenness can hinder a divine encounter in prayer. All of us need forgiveness, and all of us must release forgiveness. The prayer model of Jesus has the component of releasing forgiveness to those who have wronged us.

There is no unforgiveness in heaven, so we must model our relationships after what we see above us, not around us. This is like the priest going to the laver (the washing bowl in the Temple) before entering in. We too must enter into His presence with clean hands and a pure heart. They have already been provided for us in the blood of Christ, but we must appropriate them each and every day as we walk with our fellow mortals. After we come clean through receiving forgiveness, we can move forward toward heaven and closer into His heart.

How do we forgive?

1. Admit the pain. Don't just stuff it deeper or think it doesn't matter. To acknowledge that someone has hurt you is the beginning of forgiveness and freedom.

2. Work through the confusion of your feelings. Sort out

your thoughts and consider that you may have had a part in the offense.

3. Set holy boundaries. When you feel your heart straying or your mind reliving the trauma, set a boundary and defend it carefully. This is watching over your own soul.

4. Turn the pain into insight. Consider what happened and ask God to teach you through it any lesson He chooses to reveal. This will bring you to the very point of extending forgiveness. Joseph had to forgive in order to be released from his prison. He forgave those who had forgotten him, devalued him, and hurt him the most.

5. Make a choice to relinquish the entire event. Give up your right to be angry. This makes forgiveness real. Our Lord Jesus, the Master of Forgiveness, shows us the higher way. To pray requires that we forgive. To pray with Jesus on the Sea of Glass requires that we forgive every offense.

"AS WE OURSELVES RELEASE FORGIVENESS TO THOSE WHO HAVE WRONGED US"

Forgive as often as you want to be forgiven. This is the lesson of this prayer. There is nothing as serious as unforgiveness in the heart. It reduces our prayers to hypocrisy. We must press in to the grace of forgiving all that offends us. We must take a pre-determined posture before the world that we will seek to be un-offendable. We decide ahead of time not to be offended by the deeds of others and to extend true forgiveness whenever we're mistreated. This is divine insulation for the heart. The evil cycle of sin—offense—is broken by an attitude of forgiveness. Curses are shattered and strongholds demolished when you forgive those who have wronged you.

"RESCUE US EVERY TIME WE FACE TRIBULATION"

This is a prayer for power to overcome sin and to be freed from the snares of life. There are temptations you may escape if you pray. Intercession builds a wall of protection around your soul. It's taking the armor of God and putting on each piece by prayer. Prayer-clothing is God's armor for the soul and will deliver us from temptation. This verse causes us to wonder how many temptations we may not have had to experience in life if we'd prayed. Every believer walks in grace, but there is a measure of "saving grace" that comes only when we intercede.

See this as a request for God not to promote us beyond what our character can handle. When God puts His hand of favor and outstanding blessing upon us, we're often led into the temptation of pride and believing we deserve the glory. This prayer preserves us from being promoted beyond the grace that would keep us humble and usable in God's hands. Our gift and responsibilities may be ready for promotion, but our character may not yet be mature and stable.

This prayer is intensified as we come together as one. Churches may pray with confidence that the health and future of the church will be preserved through corporate intercession. In these difficult days of world tension and pressure on all sides, it's so crucial that the church comes together to say to God our Father, "rescue *us* every time we face tribulation."

"AND SET US FREE FROM EVIL"

It's clear that intercession thwarts demonic strategies. True deliverance from the evil one who walks this earth can only be secured as we intercede with others. The little word *us* is repeated throughout the Lord's Prayer to show us that it's corporate intercession that's in view here. A church that neglects having consistent, regular prayer meetings can expect to get "beat up" by the evil one. Prayer secures us from the schemes of the enemy.

The word *evil* speaks of everything that the curse of sin has brought to earth. The Greek word for *evil* is *poneros*, which is taken from a root word meaning *pain*. Jesus has destroyed the power of evil—sin, sickness, pain, and poverty (the word *evil* is derived from the Greek word *penes*, which means *poor*)—through His redemptive work on the cross for us.

There is additional help for this kind of prayer found in Psalm 91. It's wise to take this Psalm and pray its contents over your church and family. To pray together as a body will increase the hedge of protection around your church. No one is wise enough or discerning enough by themselves to detect every scheme of satan. We must have each other and enter into corporate prayer. Not a pastor, prophet, nor apostle is enough, but all of us must pray as one, asking in unity that the favor of God will "set us free from evil."

"FOR YOU ARE THE KING WHO RULES WITH POWER AND GLORY FOREVER. AMEN!"

Prayer will always acknowledge the power and glory as belonging to God alone. They're His possessions, and they're His to give. It's when we acknowledge that they belong to Him that He releases them to us. As we move into the declarations of praise, heaven pours into the earth. When we act as though the power and glory belong to or originate with us, we are left empty. When we bow before Sovereignty, we leave with wealth.

The Lord's Prayer is for our intercession. We can ask for the nations to receive the revelation of salvation. Our inheritance is to be the conversion of nations, not just our neighborhood (Psalm 2:8; Isaiah 55:5). Both Paul and Peter prayed for the understanding of salvation for all men (1 Timothy 2:1–8; 2 Peter 3:8–9).

We can believe things we cannot even imagine. Then we can go further! Your faith needs stretching. Holy Spirit prayers will go further than your imagination (Ephesians 3:18–21). Your prayers should go beyond your thoughts and comprehension. The future belongs to the intercessors who believe the future into being. Through your prayers, an alternative future may happen as you pull the will of God down to the earth.

When we grow desperate enough, passionate enough, and prayerful enough, the Lord will answer our cry, and the church will become His throne of grace upon the earth! We can expect great answers to our prayers. This is the hour of destiny for planet Earth. The Scriptures will soon be fulfilled. May this be the generation of those who seek His face. We have been given privileges that even the angels don't have. There is no record of angels of heaven praying. It's time for us to ask, seek, and knock!

Pray this today: Our heavenly Father, may the glory of your name be the center on which our life turns. May your Holy Spirit come upon us and cleanse us. Manifest your kingdom on earth. And give us our needed bread for the coming day. Forgive our sins as we ourselves release forgiveness to those who have wronged us. And rescue us every time we face tribulations. Amen

12

THE PRAYER WARRIOR

In every battle, take faith as your wrap-around shield, for it is able to extinguish the blazing arrows coming at you from the Evil One! Embrace the power of salvation's full deliverance, like a helmet to protect your thoughts from lies. And take the mighty razor-sharp Spirit-sword of the spoken Word of God. Pray passionately in the Spirit, as you constantly intercede with every form of prayer at all times. Pray the blessings of God upon all his believers.

EPHESIANS 6:16–18

Prayer warriors are the most powerful world-changing beings on earth. They know who they are. They're the children of God, and they act like it! They never wonder about the future because they are too busy creating it through their faith in God.

Paul wrote:

I pray that you will continually experience the immeasurable greatness of God's power made available to you through faith. Then your lives will be an advertisement of this immense power as it works through you! This is the mighty power that was released when God raised Christ from the dead and exalted him to the place of highest honor and supreme authority in the heavenly realm! (Ephesians 1:19–20).

If you are a Christian, there's a power accompanying your life that's greater than great! It's the "immeasurable greatness of His power." It's not human power, but the actual "greatest of God's power," "the strength of His might." Think about it: The immeasurable power of God Almighty is attached to your prayer life! The power of God's might is His resurrection power. What does resurrection mean? It means that things which look dead, smell dead, and act dead can be touched by God and raised to life! This is the mighty power that was released when God raised Christ from the dead and exalted Him to the place of highest honor and supreme authority in the heavenly realm (Ephesians 1:20).

Right now, you have resurrection power attached to your prayer life that can absolutely speak to things that are dead and call forth eternal life! The power in us is the same potency God demonstrated when He raised Jesus out of the grave—His resurrection power. Our mission is to bring resurrection life to situations that are dead.

If the devil challenges your prayer, remind him that you're seated with Christ, "and he is exalted as first above every ruler, authority, government and realm of power in existence! He is gloriously enthroned over every name that is praised, not only in this age, but in the age that is coming!" (Ephesians 1:21). Christ's authority is final. For not only has the Father put "everything beneath His authority," but He "has given Him the highest rank above all others.

And now we, his church, are his body on the earth and that which fills him who is being filled by it!" (Ephesians 1:22–23).

This is a most profound understanding of our role: What Christ has attained, we carry out here on the earth. God has positioned the church as the living bridge between the terrible conditions on earth and the wonderful solutions from heaven! As we truly, passionately, and accurately submit to Christ in prayer, the kingdom of heaven steadily enters our world. The key, of course, is to know Christ's Word. We have the authority of the Word of God! As we receive the revelation, join our prayers with the Word, and persevere in prayer, we will see the future conformed to God's will here on earth!

Jesus told a parable in Luke 18:1–8 teaching us to never stop praying or lose hope. In other words, if you're not praying, you will lose heart. For most of the things we pray about, we must persevere and pray through to get the answer. Prayer anchors us in God's strength for each battle in life that we face. We know that it works just by the very fact that we were converted. We were saved because someone went to battle for us! As we look on our own miracle of conversion, we can gain confidence in God's help to transform others.

Jesus said, "What seems impossible to you is never impossible to God!" (Matthew 19:26). Under that banner, we pray and believe God. The Holy Spirit ever lives to make intercession. All we need to do is open our hearts to Him and allow Him to fill us with overcoming faith. Then we must watch as the impossible becomes possible!

Look at the terrible issues of our world right now. Every need we see is where God wants us to release prayer to see His outcome for that situation. God shows us what's wrong so we can pray for things to be made right. Why waste energy criticizing what's wrong when our prayers can change it? The Lord our God, who is in the midst of us, is mighty. Our weapons of warfare (the Word of God and the prayers of faith) are mighty to pull down the strongholds. Stop thinking of yourself as unable to pray. That's a lie out of hell. You were destined to pray mighty prayers!

MADE STRONG IN OUR WEAKNESS

> For although we live in the natural realm we don't wage a military campaign employing human weapons, using manipulation to achieve our aims. Instead, our spiritual weapons are energized with divine power to effectively dismantle the defenses behind which people hide. We can demolish every deceptive fantasy that opposes God and break through every arrogant attitude that is raised up in defiance of the true knowledge of God. We capture, like prisoners of war, every thought and insist that it bow in obedience to the Anointed One. (2 Corinthians 10:3–5)

Many try to move heaven without touching heaven with a devotional life in God. But the Lord is looking for intimate lovers, not just warriors. A life of intimate devotion and seeking the Father's heart daily is necessary for our prayers to be effective and potent. To forget about this is to forget that you have an enemy who will take advantage of every weakness. Jehoshaphat's strategy for warfare was to worship out of weakness (2 Chronicles 20:21). When we're weak, we're strong (2 Corinthians 12:7–10). True power for warfare is not because we are gifted, experienced, or clever. It's because we have a great King and God who lives within us! Worshipping God in His holiness will protect us in every battle.

Unless we believers appreciate our weaknesses, we will be deceived. Our blind spots become targets. Our strengths will become places where pride leads us astray. We commit a fatal blunder when we think we are beyond the control or manipulation of an evil spirit. When a child of God becomes "spiritual" (Galatians 6:1) he/she is subject to the influence of the supernatural world. This is why Paul first mentions the need to be "strong in the Lord and in His mighty power" before instructing us of our armor (Ephesians 3:16; 6:10). If we think the armor is our strength, we'll fail. His mighty power living in us wins the battle in prayer.

After Jesus gave His disciples the power and the authority to cast out demons and heal the sick (Luke 9:1–3), He gave them one parting word: "Take nothing extra on your journey. Just go as you are. Don't carry a staff, a backpack, food, money, not even a change of clothes" (Luke 9:3). Why would He tell them to take nothing? Because He had given them all they needed! His power and authority, and nothing else, must be our strength.

Grace is enough to take with us on our prayer journey. We need only the realization that it's God plus nothing. When we're content to be the nothing, God can and will flow through us in prayer (Romans 8:26). It's not that we take no "things" with us; it's that we realize that what we have in grace is more than sufficient to sustain us.

When grace makes us strong, passion keeps us faithful. To be passionate is to be awakened to the mission of bringing Christ into our environment. I believe that every believer must be passionate or they will sink into passivity. Nothing can give more ground to the enemy in your life than a passive spirit! Always remember your authority, and never back down! Remember that you're seated in the heavenly realm and in the throne room when you pray. So

P.U.S.H.: Pray Until Something Happens! Mighty is the One who is in you! There's an English word for what happens when you don't resist the enemy—it's called depression! Your muscles will only grow stronger as you battle the adversary and push back. You will no longer be depressed; you'll be energized to pray, knowing that your prayers are weapons in God's hands (Psalm 18:32–45).

PREPARING AN AREA FOR BREAKTHROUGH

Jesus sent out seventy disciples (seventy-two disciples in the NIV) to preach the gospel, heal the sick, and cast out demons. Miracle-working power was released through the disciples pulling down strongholds in heaven and breaking open the way for Christ to follow!

> After this, the Lord Jesus formed thirty-five teams among the other disciples. Each team was two disciples, seventy in all, and he commissioned them to go ahead of him into every town he was about to visit. He released them with these instructions: "The harvest is huge and ripe. But there are not enough harvesters to bring it all in. As you go, plead with the Owner of the Harvest to drive out into his harvest fields many more workers." (Luke 10:1–2)

Jesus sent His disciples ahead to the very places that He Himself was about to go to release His miracle ministry. The release of the seventy was not just sending out preachers; it was the release of a highly anointed and strategic takeover of the demonic influence over a region. This strategy would precede the personal appearance of Jesus Himself in these specific cities.

The famous revivalist Charles Finney used this same strategy. He would always send Father Nash into town. And Nash would gather a team of two or three to covenant their hearts together, and, with throne room prayer, they would release heaven in each region. After they had prepared the way, Finney would go in and preach the gospel, reaping a great harvest of souls. It was the same way that Jesus operated. It was as though the seventy were the "breakers" (Micah 2:13). They opened the way, and Jesus came behind to completely mop up the enemy's camp. But of course, Jesus was the real breaker, working in tandem with His disciples, His prayer partners!

As they were sent, they were given the task of interceding for "laborers" to be sent into the harvest. Jesus was giving them an example of a strategy that could be repeated by a massive and coordinated spiritual assault in a region of apostolic ministry. And could it be that the "laborers" are really those released in battle formation like the seventy? This is an example of a strategically released force of "laborers" into a region. They'll be those that have spent time in the throne room and have been anointed to break the network of power over the area: men and women who are anointed as sent ones to prepare the way of the Lord and bring in the harvest!

There is a golden bowl of prayer in the heavenly realm that the church must fill:

> And when the twenty-four elders and the four living creatures saw the Lamb had taken the scroll, they fell facedown at the feet of the Lamb and worshiped him. Each of them had a harp and golden bowls brimming full of sweet fragrant incense—which are the prayers of God's holy lovers. (Revelation 5:8)

Then the eighth angel with a golden incense burner came and took his place at the incense altar. He was given a great quantity of incense to offer up, consisting of the prayers of God's holy people, upon the golden altar that is before the throne. And the smoke of the incense with the prayers of the holy ones billowed up before God from the hand of the angel. (Revelation 8:3–4)

Every time the saints gather to intercede, the golden bowl of intercession begins to fill. As this bowl runs over and is poured out, revival power begins to flow. God waits until the bowl is full before He picks it up in His hand and pours it out. Every church has a bowl to fill. Are you actively filling your bowl of intercession? Your prayers are a sweet incense to Jesus. Let Him inhale it!

Pray this today: Lord Jesus, I delight to spend time in prayer with you. I find my strength in you. I take the whole armor of God and place it on my mind and my spirit today. I will face the enemy unafraid, for I am robed in your splendor. I will be your prayer warrior today and win every battle in the name of my God. Amen.

13

WEAPONS FROM THE THRONE ROOM

By the power of God working through us,
and with the mighty weapons of righteousness—
a sword in one hand and a shield in the other.

2 CORINTHIANS 6:7

As you come to God in believing prayer on behalf of others, there will be times when you'll face the powers of darkness. But there are mighty weapons in the throne room at your disposal. Your destiny is to tear down strongholds wherever you find them. And when you do, you'll be loosing others to fulfill their destiny. You're seated in heavenly places and are more than a match for the devil because Jesus lives in you!

Your arsenal is complete. God has given you every weapon you need for warfare and intercessory authority. Your part is to appropriate these weapons with courage. God's Word guarantees your victory! The heavenly believer knows how to use the Word of God and how to listen to the Holy Spirit of God to break down the enemy's lies. For it's the Mighty Jesus living within you that strikes terror in their hearts. We take up the weapons of heaven and abandon the "weapons of the world," which include:

- Human reasoning—Our own thinking
- Praying our desires—Forcing our will or arguments upon others
- Manipulation—Using the fear of rejection on others
- Deception—Any distortion of the truth for our own ends
- Control—Binding others emotionally to ourselves

Our weapons are spiritual and mighty to the pulling down of strongholds! We can blast through strongholds with prophetic prayers and proclamations. We can decree and declare with shouts of triumph. We have the angelic presence that goes before us even as the Angel of the Lord went ahead of Israel as they came out of Egypt (Exodus 23:20–23). When we pray in agreement with the will of God, the enemy will give up. Our high praises will become God's bulldozers to level the walls that hold the church captive. These are our weapons of Throne Room Prayer!

FAITH AND OBEDIENCE—OUR FOUNDATION

The foundation of spiritual warfare is faith and obedience. Faith is essential in crushing doubt, fear, and darkness. Without faith, you can't please God or conquer the enemy. When you take the name of Jesus, His Blood, and the Word of God and mix them with faith, you have the greatest arsenal in the universe. The very power of God flows through your faith. It's your victory, your shield, and your boldness (Mark 11:22–24; 1 John 5:4, Ephesians 6:16; Hebrews 10:22). When you face accusations from the enemy or any opposition to your spiritual advance, faith must rise in your spirit. Faith rests in truth, accusation in lies. Believe the truth of God, resist the devil in faith, and you will see the enemy run (1 Peter 5:9).

These twin virtues of faith and obedience are our pillars for victory. They're intertwined and work together and each is incomplete without the other. They are the two things that activate all the weapons. Your very life must be a statement of faith and obedience to the kingdom of darkness or you will retreat in the face of their fury! God tells us that we have been given "a sword in one hand and a shield in the other" as weapons of righteousness (2 Corinthians 6:7). Faith in the Word of God and obedience to the Word of God are those righteous weapons.

The Name of Jesus—Our Authority

Everything must bow before the name of Jesus! It's the one and only name that has power on earth, in heaven, and in hell! You can use the name of Jesus as though He Himself, with all of His authority, is standing beside you (1 Corinthians 6:17). King Jesus has given you the authority and power over demons, and you have the right to ask the Father for victory in His name (Luke 10:19). John 14:13–14 gives us one of the major weapons from the throne room—the name of Jesus: "For I will do whatever you ask me to do when you ask me in my name. And that is how the Son will show what the Father is really like and bring glory to him. Ask me anything in my name, and I will do it for you!" Use the name/names of Jesus in warfare as you intercede! Power and virtue are represented by that name. God recognizes that name and will answer you. And the demons recognize that name and tremble (Psalm 18:45). Make the enemy flee in terror! Speak the name of Jesus over the strongholds of darkness. Use this weapon, beloved! The power of the Holy Spirit is released when you take up the name/names of Jesus.

This can be likened to a police officer who's wearing his badge and using the authority behind that badge to stop vehicles many times larger than himself. In the same way, intercessors who wear the badge of the name of Jesus can stop the schemes of satan, unlock the power of God, and release His authority in every place you encounter darkness.

We are using the revelation of who God is when we use His name on our battlefield. Inner fears and crippling doubts flee when we understand who God is. At His name, angels bow, demons flee, and hardened hearts melt. The climax of human history will be the unveiling of the glory of the name of Jesus! His name is great and greatly to be praised (Philippians 2:5–10).

However, there is a warning attached to using the name of Jesus: To have authority in the Spirit to use this name requires an intimate and personal relationship with Him. Your fellowship with Jesus in secret gives you power over darkness. To use the name of Jesus as a "good luck charm" will get you into trouble! It is not enough to use the name of Jesus; we must have the nature of Jesus in our hearts. If your life is in disobedience or compromise, you're using God's name in vain. Power comes from relationship. Peter and James used the name of Jesus to heal the lame man at the Gate Beautiful (Acts 3:1–8). They were known as men who had been with Jesus and absorbed His life. The glory of His name is seen in the fruit of His life coming from you.

The "seven sons of Sceva" tried to use the name of Jesus

without a relationship with Him. They were beaten and bruised by demons (Acts 19:11–17). How many times have you been beaten and bruised by the enemy? Could it be that you were praying in the name of Jesus with hidden compromise in your life? Authority and power flow through relationship. Under His shadow, we cast down strongholds. Apart from Him, we can do nothing.

THE BLOOD OF JESUS—OUR COVERING

We have representation in heaven at the highest level by His blood. Our Great High Priest has brought His sacred blood before the Father's throne and purchased our boldness. We're not uncovered or vulnerable as we pray. We're covered in the blood of Christ.

The subject of the blood of Jesus in Scripture is astonishing. From Genesis to Revelation, God has used the blood of innocence to atone, cover, and remove guilt. Where guilt has been removed, power flows! The blood of Jesus, like the blood of the Passover lamb, drives away the death angel (Exodus 12:22–23). Dark powers are stripped of their weapons where the blood of Jesus is applied.

The blood of Jesus is His life in sacrifice before the Father. The life is in the blood. The shed blood of His cross releases the indestructible and endless life of Jesus. It cannot be overcome. The blood of God conquers dark princes. One drop of His blood had enough power to redeem all of humanity from the chains of sin. Imagine how the demons see the blood. Here are eight things the blood of Jesus does for you:

1. The blood saves us—Ephesians 1:7

2. The blood justifies us before God—Acts 13:38–39

3. The blood sanctifies us—Hebrews 10:10,14

4. The blood reconciles us to God—Colossians 1:20

5. The blood has overcoming power—Luke 10:19;
   Revelation 12:11

6. The blood cleanses us from all sin—1 John 1:7

7. The blood releases new covenant power—Hebrews
   7:22; 8:13

8. The blood delivers us from darkness—Colossians
   1:13–14; 2:15

To use the blood of Jesus in warfare and intercession is to stand identified with the complete acceptance of the Lamb. The perfections, the glory, the life, and the righteousness of the Lamb of God is conveyed in the blood. This weapon will never fail. To apply the blood of Jesus is to remind the enemy of his boundaries, failures, and weaknesses.

The blood of Jesus does to the enemy what a lie of accusation does to you! Give it back to him! Remind the enemy of the power of the blood! Push him back with the crimson wave of power, the blood of the precious Son of God! In the fiercest fight against the dark forces, the blood of Jesus will work for you. This overcoming power is at your disposal, and you're safe in the "bubble" of the blood! How grateful we are that Jesus loved us more than His own blood.

Pray this today: Lord Jesus, there is no one like you! Your love has broken through and brought me into the beautiful chamber room of the King! Although at times I feel weak and feeble, being with you on the Sea of Glass changes everything. I draw my strength from you, my Lord. I am more than a conqueror through you and through your endless love. Thank you, my King! Amen.

14

MORE WEAPONS FROM THE THRONE ROOM

For we have the living Word of God, which is full of energy—
like a two-mouthed sword. It will even penetrate to the very core
of our being where soul and spirit, bone and marrow meet!
It interprets and reveals the true thoughts and secret motives of
our hearts. There is not one person who can hide their thoughts
from God, for nothing that we do remains a secret, and nothing
created is concealed, but everything is exposed and defenseless
before his eyes, to whom we must render an account.

HEBREWS 4:12-13

It's impossible to overstate the importance of the Word of God in our prayer life. Words are the containers of our faith. They're powerful enough to pull down the enemies' strongholds and to demolish them. We're in combat with demonic darkness, but because the Word of God dwells richly in us, we have ample ammunition to discharge against any attack. As the Word of God comes from our mouths, it has a dramatic impact on the spirit realm around us.

The Scripture above states that God's Word is full of energy—like a two-mouthed sword. Many translations read, "like a two-edged sword," but the Greek word is actually "mouth." His Word is like a sword coming from two mouths, God's and ours! Our mouth is filled with God's truth, and we speak it out in declaration; it becomes a two-mouthed sword! How important it is to be filled with the Word of God and be filled with the Holy Spirit.

There is power for spiritual dominion against the enemy in the words we pray! Everything you do in intercession and spiritual warfare must be based on the Word of God. His Word abiding in you gives you wisdom for warfare, strength for the battle, and faith to combat your foe (John 15:7–8). You must learn to use the Word of God as a sword against dark powers (Ephesians 6:17). The more you know and confess the Word, the more effective will be your victory. Here are some ways you can use the sword of the Spirit:

- Allow the Spirit to use the Word as a sword in your own heart first.
- Quote the Word to the enemy and remind him of his defeat.
- Quote the Word to the Lord to affirm His promises.
- Ask God for a word of direction for the person or situation.

Ignorance of the Word of God will leave you defenseless. Jesus, the incarnate Word, used the written Word when He was tempted by the devil. If Jesus needed the Word, then so do we. The Bible is full of ammunition for warfare. Just look at all the promises of God, the prophetic prayers, the apostolic teachings, and the book of Revelation.

The History of Israel

Exodus, Joshua, and Judges give us incredible insight into battlefield strategies. The name *Joshua* is the Old Testament form of the name *Jesus*. You can read through the books of Joshua and Judges as though they were manuals for spiritual warfare! Take note of the different strategies God released to His leaders for war. Note their defeats as well as their victories. Everything written is for our example and instruction (1 Corinthians 10:6, 11).

Joshua 10 is perhaps the most powerful example of spiritual warfare and intercessory prayer in the Word. This chapter records the epic battle between the Israelites and the five kings of the Amorites. After an all-night march, Joshua took his enemies by surprise. And the Lord helped with the artillery of heaven! Hailstones fell from the sky as Joshua executed judgment on his enemies! More were killed by the hailstones than by the swords of the Israelites. And with the declaration of Joshua, the sun stood still so that the warfare could be completed! I fully believe that in these last days, the Lord will be working miracles so astounding that they will be compared to the book of Joshua.

His Word Worked for Me

The "word of their testimony" of Revelation 12:11 are the specific truths of God that have delivered the saints. Each one of us can say that our testimony is that the Word of God worked for us! There is no victory apart from the Lord and His Word. The word of our testimony is the word we use to testify of God's power! Here is a sample word of testimony that is sure to push back the devil:

- I testify that the Word of God has set me free!
- I stand before you covered and sprinkled in the precious blood of Christ.
- Through the blood of Christ, I have been redeemed from the hand of the enemy.
- Through the blood, all my sins have been forgiven and I am continually cleansed from sin.
- Through the blood of Jesus, I am set apart for the Father.
- I carry His authority and the enemy has no place in me.
- My body is the temple of the Holy Spirit!
- The enemy has no power over me for the blood of Jesus has been shed for me!

PRAISE AND WORSHIP—OUR BANNER

Praise and worship are such effective tools for fighting our battles. They open the heavenly realm for revelation, power, and God's Spirit to flow. As we praise, the prison doors of our soul open and we are set free again (Acts 16:23–26). Jesus taught His disciples to begin and end prayer with praise.

We don't wait to worship God until we have the victory—as we worship, the victory comes! We do battle from a place of victory with praise as the ground of victory beneath our feet. Put on your garments of praise and watch what the Father does in your heart and through your prayers!

When you clap your hands or lift them in praise, you're waging war in the heavens and loosing havoc on the enemy's kingdom.

Don't neglect to use prophetic worship in your gatherings and in your devotional times as well. Prophetic worship is such a powerful weapon when you're facing an enemy in the spirit. When you don't know what to do, ask the Lord and prophetically praise your way into victory. Praise and worship will win your battles!

Praise releases captives and brings in a harvest. Your worship will not only set you free, but it will set the hearts of others free as well. When God sent King Jehoshaphat into battle, He armed him with a song: "Let everyone thank God, for He is good, and He is easy to please! His tender love for us continues on forever!" As we sing, our music becomes a weapon for God to wield from His heavenly throne room. And when we lift our hearts to Him in song, heavenly foes will be conquered (Isaiah 30:32). "No wonder the peoples praise you! Let all the peoples praise you more! The harvest of the earth is here! God, the very God we worship, keeps us satisfied at His banquet of blessings" (Psalm 67:5–6).

Worship and intercession are powerful as they flow together to dismantle strongholds in the heavenly places. This is the ministry of the harp and bowl described in the heavenly scene of Revelation 5:8–9:

> And when the twenty-four elders and the four living creatures saw the Lamb had taken the scroll, they fell face-down at the feet of the Lamb and worshiped Him. Each of them had a harp and golden bowls brimming full of sweet fragrant incense—which are the prayers of God's holy lovers. And they were all singing this new song of praise to the Lamb.

This is the mingling of worship and intercession that results in the demolishing of strongholds in the kingdom of darkness.

How does Praise Help Us Defeat the Enemy?

- It draws you into His presence where you can receive wisdom and strength—Psalm 100:4

- It releases the activity of the throne room on your behalf—Isaiah 60:18

- It paralyzes the forces of darkness and defeats the enemy—2 Kings 11:13–14; Psalm 8:2; 149:5–9

- It hastens revival—2 Chronicles 31:2; 34:12; Psalm 107:32

- Praise is God's address. When we praise, we are brought into His house—Psalm 22:3

- Praise is the garment you wear; it clothes you in the Spirit—Isaiah 61:1–3

- It is the way into Christ's victory—Psalm 106:47; 2 Corinthians 2:14

- Praise is a sacrifice we offer to God—Jeremiah 33:11; Hebrews 13:15

Pray this today: Father God, I need you. I want to be an intercessor, a prayer warrior, one who will join you in the rulership of the universe one day. You have given me mighty weapons from your throne room. Help me to use them boldly and without fear, for I am yours and you are mine. Amen.

15

BREAKTHROUGH PRAYER

"You are my righteous Father, but the unbelieving world has never known you, in the perfect way that I know you! And all those who believe in me also know that you have sent me. I have revealed to them who you are and I will continue to make you even more real to them, so that they may experience the same endless love that you have for me, for your love will now live in them, even as I live in them."

JOHN 17:25–26

The greatest prayer of all time is found in John 17. It was the prayer of our Magnificent Intercessor, Jesus Christ, spoken in the garden of Gethsemane on the night He was betrayed. Knowing He was going to be delivered up that night to be condemned and crucified, He spent His last night on earth interceding for us. This is the most prophetic prayer in the Scriptures. It is a prayer that will yet be answered by God the Father for His end-time church. The Father Himself is committed to answering the prayer of His dear Son, and every request in this prayer will be fulfilled before Jesus returns.

Jesus prayed the breakthrough prayer for you! No one has interceded like Jesus Christ for His beloved bride, the church. Flaming zeal in His heart prompted Him to pray for you before He was crucified. You were in His mind the night He was betrayed. Desire for you to know the Father filled His soul. Ponder this prayer found in John 17. Pray it over a few times and allow the Holy Spirit to give you understanding. It's time for a new level of prayer to arise in the church of the nations. Aggressive, powerful, passionate, glorious breakthrough prayer!

BREAKTHROUGH PRAYER IS *PROPHETIC*

> "If they are prophets and have the word of the LORD, let them plead with the LORD Almighty." (Jeremiah 27:18 NIV)

A radical new breed of humble, broken-hearted intercessors is rising up in the church. They are powerfully prophetic and have learned how to touch the heart of God. Many are hidden in secret and are praying night and day for revival, righteousness, the destiny of nations, churches, and leaders. It's time for the "Anna company" to arise and pray the prophetic promises back to God! Anna was a hidden but significant prophetic intercessor who was on hand when Jesus was offered in dedication as an infant. Extravagantly devoted for as much as sixty years to intercession in the house of the Lord, she was one praying widow! As one who dwelt in the secret place of intimacy with God, she was made aware of the times of transition and the appearing of the Christ. She'll have a place in history as one who waited, prayed, and believed until the Promise came.

We see her at eighty-four years old, still seeking God fervently

(Luke 2:36–38). There had to be a burning passion in her heart to keep her praying in the temple all those years. There's no record of any prophecy she spoke, but she was a woman of the secret place.

The expression of her prophetic ministry was in her enduring intercession for the redemption of Jerusalem. She prayed through the prophetic promises of God. She was given revelation, and she prayed until she saw it fulfilled. Praying prophets are anointed to bring change in the spiritual climate around them. Though not limited to women, this company of kingdom-pullers seem to follow in the steps of Anna. They give birth, travail, and labor in prayer. This is their call and their joy.

These prayer partners with Jesus see with heavenly eyes and pray until His will is done. They've entered into the intercessory ministry of Jesus Christ. Seated with Him, they see from His viewpoint and their intercession flows from revelation. Their prayers become swords and weapons. It may begin by something as simple as a burden to pray. And yet, the burden will remain until they pray it through. This was God's prayer assignment for them.

The heart of the intercessor becomes the "womb" where God's purpose labors to be born. The intercessor becomes a focused warrior, conspiring[2] with God to release His glory on the earth! The prophetic intercessors seen in the Old Testament include Abraham, Esther, Daniel, Deborah, Joseph, Jeremiah, and more. Ask the Lord, *Is this my call? Is that what you're drawing me into?*

BREAKTHROUGH PRAYER IS *POWERFUL*

The church of Jesus Christ is returning to the fire and passion of the first century church. This "apostolic move" of God has begun to take hold in the earth, bringing renewal and restoration

---

[2] The word *conspire* means "to breathe together."

to the foundations of the churches. Fresh revelation for relevant preaching is pouring out from the Word of God. And a fiery, passionate form of prayer has been birthed in our day that will unlock the heavens over nations and cities.

It is breakthrough prayer, authoritative and powerful, that brings a shift in the heavens. This type of prayer has momentum and spiritual force. It blasts through the defenses of the enemy and results in accomplishing the will of God. The advance of the kingdom of heaven is a matter of intense conflict. It's the imposition of a superior force on this darkened planet. Every aspect of the kingdom of God is a threat to satan. There is no advance without his opposition and resistance. But God's kingdom will never retreat. It operates in one gear only—forward.

Boldness terrifies the devil. It speaks of a divine power and a spiritual impartation that gives authority to whatever is spoken. Our words become breakers to rip open the atmosphere that hinders God's advance. It's a determination to match fire with fire and not back down from the intimidation of principalities and powers. These powerful apostolic decrees will be heard again through the lips of kingdom advancers and prophetic declarers. Our governmental prayers release the nuclear power of demonic destruction.

BREAKTHROUGH PRAYER IS *GOVERNMENTAL*

Breakthrough prayer shifts things in the heavens and moves things on earth. Joshua was a man who prayed governmental, breakthrough prayers. He was one who matched fire with fire, and his bold prayer changed human history. God listened to the voice of a man and stopped the sun. Joshua's voice was a cry and a decree meant to avenge the enemies of God and destroy their stronghold over the land. It's the highest level of breakthrough prayer recorded in the Bible besides the prayers of Jesus. Joshua's prayer released God to fight with man. This partnership-prayer gave the earth a display of explosive power like it had never seen before. The skies opened up, and God sent hailstones crashing down to the earth on the heads of His enemies. Joshua chased them, but God sent the hailstones. Man and God fought together with breakthrough anointing (Joshua 10:12–14).

Caught up in the momentum of the purposes of God, Joshua tapped into the awesome faith that took him far outside the boundaries of the natural. He commanded the physical universe to heed the call of God and hear the voice of His servant. Because Joshua shared God's heart and zeal for victory, the miracle came! Breakthrough prayer is always rooted in the passions of God and will break boundaries and decree a thing until it is done.

It's time to take prayer to the breakthrough level, the place of divine response. We must not be content to leave our prayer life on the religious level of merely something that we must do to be spiritual. When David prayed, the heavens shook and the voice of God was clearly heard.

> I cried out to you in my distress, the delivering God,
> and from your temple-throne you heard my troubled cry.
> My sobs came right into your heart
> and you turned your face to rescue me.
> The earth itself shivered and shook.
> It reeled and rocked before him.
> As the mountains trembled, they melted away!
> For his anger was kindled, burning on my behalf.
> Fierce flames leapt from his mouth,
> erupting with blazing, burning coals as smoke
> and fire encircled him.

He stretched heaven's curtain open and came to my defense.
Swiftly he rode to earth as the stormy sky was lowered.
He rode a chariot of thunderclouds amidst thick darkness,
a cherub his steed as he swooped down,
soaring on the wings of Spirit-wind.
Wrapped and hidden in the thick-cloud darkness,
his thunder-tabernacle surrounded him.
He hid himself in mystery-darkness;
the dense rain clouds were his garments.
Suddenly the brilliance of his presence broke through
with lightning bolts and with a mighty storm from heaven—
like a tempest dropping coals of fire.
The Lord thundered, the great God above every god
spoke with his thunder-voice from the skies.
What fearsome hailstones and flashes of fire were before him!
(Psalm 18:6–13)

This kind of prayer stirs God to move and uncover the hidden things. God races upon the wings of the wind to break through and create the miracle prayed for. Every time your prayer is answered, God mounts the cherubim and thunders His decrees from heaven on your behalf. The results we see in the natural world are only the outer wrapping of the power He displays in the spirit realm in response to our urgent prayer.

In the early days of the church, the evil King Herod came against the body of Christ. He sought to throw Peter in prison in hopes that it would paralyze the church. He recognized Peter's anointing and authority so he had Peter seized and then had him guarded by sixteen soldiers. When word reached the church, they immediately entered into "intense intercession" to secure his release. The Greek word used in Acts 12:5 for *intense intercession* is literally "stretching out in prayer." It's the word from which we get the English word *tension*. It means to "stretch out in prayer with a tension" in our activity. It is prayer that stretches the boundaries and vibrates the spiritual realm until something pops, something gives, and something breaks through!

In seasons of stretching prayer, the saints pray with intensity until the enemy yields and God's purposes stand. The saints who prayed in Acts 12 knew that Peter's deliverance in the natural was unlikely and probably would never happen. They also knew that Herod intended to either keep Peter in prison for the rest of his life or murder him. But the believers in Mary's house had a secret weapon, a stretching prayer that could change physical reality and bring a heavenly breakthrough. They broke through so Peter could break out! They wouldn't let up until God answered! And answer He did in a dramatic and powerful way!

When their prayers finally broke through, they were totally unaware, so they just kept up the tension, stretching their souls out! They had no way of knowing that a miracle had taken place until Peter turned up outside the door! Their prayers created a new reality on earth, breaking through the natural boundaries (prison doors) and releasing the miracle power they had asked for. Their insistent stretching accomplished the work, and it even took them by surprise! This is the type of prayer we must take hold of! No more boring prayer times and half-hearted whimperings. A holy hum begins to rise as the saints "stretch out in prayer," causing miracles to break loose!

Pray this today: Loving Father, I come to you today for supernatural strength. You have broken through my pain, issues, and failures, and brought me into victory. I want to linger here with you on the Sea of Glass and pour out my heart to you. No one cares for me like you do, and no one answers prayer like you do. Thank you, Father, for being my Safe Place and my High Tower. I hide myself in you today. Amen.

16

APOSTOLIC PRAYER

"So now, Lord, listen to their threats to harm us. Empower us as your servants, to speak the word of God freely and courageously. Stretch out your hand of power through us to heal, and to move in signs and wonders by the name of your holy Son, Jesus!"
At that moment the earth shook beneath them, causing the building they were in to tremble. Each one of them was filled with the Holy Spirit, and they proclaimed the word of God with unrestrained boldness.

ACTS 4:29–31

It is time to stretch the boundaries of prayer and break limitations off our prayers. God wants to restore the apostolic prayer model to the church of today. Believers need to pray big, bold, believing prayers in order to see miracles released on earth. When we join with Jesus on the Sea of Glass, we will hear the decrees and thunders of the Throne Room. The sounds of heaven are ready to cascade over the earth as our prayers open portals into heaven.

We must pray in the apostolic model left to us by the apostles of the Lamb. New Testament prayers are focused and specific. Generic, non-specific prayers really accomplish little. As we search the New Testament, we discover some valuable lessons for our prayer life from Paul and all of the apostles. They spent their lives in the Word of God and praying for the needs of all the churches (Acts 6:4). We must also value the Word of God and prayer. Only then will we have a satisfying prayer life that is filled with intercession for others.

Kingdom-advancing people have a mind-set that's clear and aggressive. They are forceful men and women who shake the status quo. The Greek word for *forceful* means to "shake violently." Their prayers shake violently the spirit realm around them because the Father has anointed them with governmental influence. Strong prayer calls down the power of the Holy Spirit and pushes kingdom reality forcefully ahead, pulling the future into now. This causes strongholds to shake and topple. Forceful men and women are coming with kingdom-advancing prayer, laying hold of its power. They plunder the kingdom of darkness and declare treason in the enemy's domain. "From the moment John stepped onto the scene until now, the realm of heaven's kingdom is bursting forth, and passionate people have taken hold of its power" (Matthew 11:12).

When the church in a region begins to cry out to God using the apostolic model, we begin to see breakthrough for our cities. The apostolic prayer model is the prayer that will break open the heavens and release revival into the cities of the earth. Paul prayed for churches in different regions to experience breakthrough. I have compiled most of the prayers found in the epistles of the New Testament and have included them below. Although there are many, take the time to look up the verses and pray them over your family, church, and region. Then watch God work!

Ephesians 1:17–19—Pray for the Holy Spirit of Wisdom and Revelation to be expressed in your life as you welcome His truth, conviction, and transforming power. Pray that every truth we learn will lead us into a deeper knowledge of Christ. Pray that hope will fill our hearts, convincing us of our destiny in Christ. And pray for the power that will overcome even death. When this prayer for the revelatory spirit to fall on the church is answered, the church will come into the fullness of His glory.

Ephesians 3:16–19—This prayer is for the supernatural strength of God to come into your being as the Holy Spirit is released within us. Faith is the virtue that will bring more of this into our lives, so pray that God will increase your faith. As you grow in love, Jesus is released from within you. Ask for His love to be revealed to you.

Ephesians 6:18–20—This is a prayer for the release of boldness and anointing for public ministry. God wants His servants to carry His Word with courage to the ends of the earth. It will require fresh measures of boldness to carry it out. Signs and wonders will be done on earth as the church moves into Holy Spirit boldness in the prayer room.

Philippians 1:9; 1 Thessalonians 3:12; 2 Thessalonians 3:5— Pray for an increase of love in the body of Christ. Only the release of the Spirit can accomplish this. He will reveal our brokenness and weaknesses that we may lean upon Him. Pray that all the gifts will flow in love as we seek the blessing of others. God will give us the wisdom of the Spirit to walk in these things.

Colossians 1:9–11—Pray that God would make known His will to His people as the Holy Spirit is released upon us. The people of God need spiritual understanding to grow and fulfill the purpose of God. Pray for power to be patient in hardships.

Colossians 4:2–4; Acts 14:27—Paul requests prayer that God would open a "door" of evangelism through the release of His anointing upon the Word. There is a door of opportunity that our prayers must knock on if we want to enter into anointed evangelism. Jesus opens these doors as we intercede in faith (Revelation 3:8). Corporate prayer must turn to the lost. Doors of opportunity swing open as the church prays. The "opening of doors" releases miracles, signs, and wonders by the Holy Spirit.

Colossians 4:12—We must pray for spiritual maturity to come to the church across the city. This type of intercession raises the level of spirituality in a region. There is a measure of grace and maturity that will only come as we pray. This brings God's will to the earth.

1 Thessalonians 3:10; 2 Corinthians 13:9; Hebrews 13:20–21; 1 Corinthians 1:8—These are prayers for the church to be established, complete, and mature. It is only by the release of the Spirit that these prayers will be answered. Spiritual fruit, gifts, and wisdom come as the Holy Spirit overwhelms our hearts with transforming grace.

Romans 15:5–6; John 17:20–22—Unity among the saints! This must be prayed down as we ask the Holy Spirit to make us one in all things. We need intercessors to pray these prayers until the leadership of the church models the unity of the Trinity.

1 Corinthians 1:4–8—Paul's apostolic prayer is for the church across a city to excel in spiritual gifts as they await the coming of Christ. Revelation knowledge and citywide strategies will be birthed. The church will grow in maturity and be blameless in the day of Christ.

2 Corinthians 13:9—This is a prayer for the church of the city to grow in maturity, wisdom, and all the dimensions of the grace of God. How right it is to pray this for your region!

1 Thessalonians 1:2–3; 2 Thessalonians 1:3—Prayers of thanksgiving for the grace given to others will bring more grace to them and enlarge our hearts in love. It's crucial that the church prays with thankful hearts as we ask for even more!

1 Thessalonians 3:9–13—The church is to pray for the release of apostolic ministry to the whole church in that region, causing the believers to abound in love and holiness. Mature ones must come and complete what is lacking and immature in the church of a region.

1 Thessalonians 5:23–25—We must pray for more passion for Jesus and purity of heart. The Holy Spirit will empower us as we pray this way. God is faithful and will be stirred to act. He will protect us and cleanse our lives and our churches.

2 Thessalonians 3:3; James 4:7—This is the closest we find to warfare praying in the New Testament. These apostolic prayers are for the power that we already possess—power to overcome, resist, and defeat dark strategies in human hearts—to be released in us. Satan, the evil one, has already been defeated in our lives and is appropriated as we pray and stand on God's promises.

2 Thessalonians 3:1–5—It will be prayer that delivers believers from persecution. Intercession digs a channel for the power and the Word of God to flow through. We must build a house of prayer in every city, asking the Father for protection from the evil one, to establish the saints, and for the love of God to be poured out.

2 Corinthians 13:7–9; 1 Thessalonians 3:10–13; Philippians 1:9—Praying these Scriptures will release the church to purity, love, and holiness. We must arise with these words in our mouths

and pull down the virtue of heaven into the bride of Christ. The bride makes herself ready when she walks in these strengths. The release of Spirit will bring this to the earth.

1 Timothy 1:17; 6:15–16—This is throne room prayer. It so pleases God's heart when we speak our blessings over Him. This is what He longs for! When we do, we're connecting with the worship going on around Him in the heavenly realm. This is connecting with eternity!

1 Timothy 2:1–4—We are given the responsibility to pray for government authorities and civil leaders. This prayer releases peace and tranquility to the church in a city. It pleases the Father that you would pray for their salvation and the salvation of all men.

2 Timothy 2:7, 24–26; Luke 24:45; Acts 16:14—We must ask God to open the hearts of others and grant them repentance. Jesus holds the keys, and prayer opens the hearts. This prayer for revelation and understanding must be a theme of our prayers.

Acts 4:24–31; Ephesians 6:19—These are prayers for boldness. There is a measure of boldness we'll never have if we don't ask for it! Boldness is a specific manifestation of the Holy Spirit that is imparted through prayer. The united prayer of apostles will release the hand of God for healing, signs, and wonders.

Matthew 9:37–38; Luke 10:2—Pray for more harvesters! The word used for "send out" in the Greek text is a lot stronger in the original text. It's the word *ekballo*, and it's used for driving or casting out demons. The Scripture tells us to plead with the owner of the harvest to *ekballo*—drive or cast out—many more workers into the harvest fields of the earth. There's a harvest waiting, and we need more of His "reaping angels." We are those "reaping angels." The Lord is going to "drive us out" to the nations of the earth to bring in the harvest. We are full of the Holy Spirit—full of His gifts, fruit, and wisdom—and the Master has need of us. The world is waiting for us to answer this prayer fully.

Romans 10:1—Pray for Israel that they would receive the knowledge of salvation in Christ. Paul earnestly prayed for Israel from his heart.

Romans 15:5-7—This is a prayer for the unity of the church within a city. The faith to unite churches in a region will be expressed by fervent intercession. We can't work it up! Only God's Spirit can answer this prayer.

Romans 15:30-33—There is a need for united, fervent prayer to secure the deliverance and freedom from persecution for those who preach the gospel. Our prayers can release safety and fruitfulness for the outreach of the gospel to go forth.

2 Thessalonians 3:1-2—Prayer multiplies the power and anointing of the spoken word. We must have an increase of power upon the preaching of the gospel and the teaching of the saints. Holy Spirit anointing increases the effectiveness.

2 Thessalonians 1:11-12—We must pray for the maturing of the church to receive a greater grace than we now have. Prayer releases heaven's substance on earth. Part of our maturing is linked to entering into our prayer partnership with Jesus.

Ephesians 3:18-19; 2 Thessalonians 3:5—This is the great prayer of Paul for an increase of the revelation of love in the churches. This deep, transforming revelation comes by the power of the Holy Spirit.

Philemon 4-6—Prayer activates evangelism. Boldness comes as the church unites in corporate prayer. As faith arises in the prayer meeting, more power and boldness is released!

Hebrews 13:20-21—This prayer acknowledges the greatness

of God, His covenant of love with us, and the power of the resurrection of Jesus. We pray out of this revelation. As we intercede, a greater level of maturity will come to the church and bring glory to our Great Shepherd.

James 1:5–6—Praying in faith releases divine wisdom. We need to ask for a walk of wisdom. We desperately need it. As we pray, true understanding and discernment flows. There is no reluctance in the Father's heart to give His kids whatever they ask for.

3 John 2—Spiritual and physical health comes to the church as we pray. Our personalities (soul) will prosper and come alive before God, reflecting the image of Christ. The God of Abraham will bless everything in our life as we intercede in His love.

Jude 20; Ephesians 6:18—We need to be praying passionately: every moment spent in the Spirit with every form of prayer is Throne Room Prayer! Answers are released, faith is built up, and boldness will rise in our midst!

17

THE HOUSE OF PRAYER

"I will welcome them into my holy mountain
And make them joyful in my house of prayer.
I will accept every sacrifice and offering
That they place on my altar,
For the house of worship will be known
As a house of prayer for all people."

ISAIAH 56:7

The Lord Jesus Christ is looking for a place to live—a place where He can dwell, not just a place to visit. He wants to come and make His dwelling among us until His church, His body is called a House of Prayer (Matthew 21:13). Wherever you find night and day prayer ascending to the Father, that's the place Jesus is going to be found. This not only brings great joy and delight to the Father's heart, but it will be enjoyable for His people as well. Enjoyable prayer is coming to a church near you! And

God will be the source and sustainer of this joy. Here are some features of enjoyable prayer:

- Prayer rooted in the assurance that God not only loves you but also enjoys you!

- It's throne-room-centered prayer flowing out of the beauteous realm of God prayed by lovesick worshippers who see God as their very great reward! It's prayer that finds its true reward in Him, not just in revival, miracles, or healing, but in Him as we see Him in His indescribable beauty (Genesis 15:1; Isaiah 4:2; 33:17).

- It's prayer based on His holiness, flowing from the throne room. It has abandoned every dark way and crooked thought. The enemy stands accusing the brethren day and night, and those accusations must be answered by night and day intercession! The church must stand before the Father in agreement. This night and day agreement will topple the strongholds of the enemy over our hearts, churches, and nation.

We are the house that Jesus built, and the gates of hell will not prevail against it! The church must be a house of prayer, a prayer center for all nations. As we pray around the clock, just watch as the harvest comes in and the Great Commission is fulfilled!

A Habitat for Divinity

From heaven's throne room, we must build a habitat for divinity! As the city church invites God to dwell in their region, the life and glory of Jesus will come. As we partner with the Lord Himself, God's highest purposes for our cities and nations will be realized. The church in each city will become a divine stronghold, a place where God's manifest presence is established. For the Lord has a burden to rivet His presence to the earth in twenty-four–hour-a-day prayer centers. These habitats for divinity will release a continuum of God's radiant presence over regions and territories of the earth.

Divine strongholds will one day be known as places where the Lord's power is manifested in healing, regional unity, extraordinary signs and wonders, and worldwide harvest. The Lord has promised to rebuild David's fallen tent, the twenty-four-hour prayer model that began on Mount Zion with an unveiled ark and God in David's backyard! This prayer model will be recaptured by the end time, and churches will fill up with worshippers and intercessory gatherings in all the major cities of the world (Acts 15:15–18).

Imagine what will happen when we begin a ministry on earth that's modeled after the ministry on the Sea of Glass! There are twenty-four elders mentioned in Revelation 4 and 5, and there are twenty-four hours in a day and twenty-four time zones around the earth. Global worship and intercession will release global harvest as we cover the earth with praise and fill the golden bowls of heaven with fragrant incense. Worship in the high place will move outward, releasing victory and triumph to the earth! Does your heart leap with joy over joining such an orchestra of worship?

WATCH AND PRAY

Words relating to watching—such as *watchmen, watchman, watch, watching, watchful, watcher,* and *watches*—are found 165 times in the Scriptures. Jesus tells us to watch *and* pray, implying that watching and praying would be distinct but similar activities. Every believer has the ministry of one who is to watch and pray. God is the one who has divinely set this before us. It's God's will to raise up faithful watchmen and to set them in place as holy sentinels for His purposes.

You must become one who watches for the Lord. We're His divinely posted lookouts who will see the enemy before he attacks. We'll be those who catch the first glimpses of the Lord as He approaches His people with revival. The cities of our land and the nations of the earth are waiting for these God-appointed watchmen to take their place. Our charge from Isaiah 62 is simply this:

- Give yourself no rest. Don't stop until the answer comes.

- Give Him no rest. We must wrestle in prayer until God lets you "pin Him down."

Our intercession is to be persistent, determined, intense, energetic, and prevailing. As God's secretaries, we remind Him of His appointments. We come before Him night and day on behalf of God's people. And the understanding of salvation is released as we pray and keep watch for the nations.

Fiery, holy intercession must be the pattern of our lives. We are to be those who make up the hedge and build up the wall in a time of battle. From Isaiah 59:16, we learn that God expects somebody to stand in the gap and rescue the oppressed—to come before Him pleading the people's case. And He is surprised when this doesn't happen. If there's no intercessor, evil and judgment may fall. Intercession turns back evil and makes a hedge of protection around the people (Psalm 94:16). The Word doesn't say that God looked for an evangelist or a pastor; He looked for an intercessor!

Our God is so eager to hear your prayers and answer them that He says in Isaiah 65:24, "Before they call I will answer; while they are still speaking I will hear." In fact, He wants us to constantly

THE HOUSE OF PRAYER

come before Him and "give Him no rest." He so loves being asked by His longing church that He sets people on the wall and appoints them to "never be silent day or night!"

God the Father is the watchman who keeps watch over the cities, nations, and peoples of the earth (Psalm 121). He watches over His Word to perform it (Jeremiah 1:12). He watches over the destinies of His beloved ones (Genesis 16:13; 28:15–21). He watches over the heavens and the earth to assure that all is going according to His plan (Psalm 33:14). He watches us when we are hurt and need a miracle (Exodus 3:16; Deuteronomy 2:7). There is no watchman like God Himself! Every wise watchman on earth has an example in Father God. We can be watchmen because He is watching! We are created in His image. And He is the chief watchman!

We find many different watchmen in the Scriptures. The Magi that came to Jesus at His birth were watchmen. They were watching the heavens for a sign. The shepherds who were watching over their flocks by night were a prophetic sign of the watchman, the Shepherd-King who would come and keep watch over His flock. And today He is calling His pastor-shepherds to keep the night watch as they guard the precious flock of Jesus.

Simeon and Anna were watching for the coming of the Lord as His parents brought Jesus to the temple to be dedicated to God. They were intercessors who fasted and prayed for eyes to see God's eternal purpose as it was brought before their eyes. What a great privilege it was for them to see and hold the baby Jesus as they gazed into the eyes of the God-Man.

At twelve years of age, Jesus was a watchman who had to be in His "Father's house" (Luke 2:49). Jesus spent His life watching the Father and doing only what He saw the Father doing. He spent nights in prayer and days in prayer. He had fellowship and communion with the one who meant the most to Him, the Father.

Jesus was the watchmen the Father looked for. Jesus was the one who would build the wall and stand before Him in the gap (Ezekiel 22:30). Jesus was the one who interceded and intervened on behalf of you and me. As we follow in His steps, we too will become watchmen on the wall.

The Lord Jesus is still wanting disciples to come alongside Him to spend a night in prayer, just as He did with Peter, James, and John in the garden of Gethsemane: "Stay here and keep watch with me" (Matthew 26:38). Jesus could sleep in a boat on a troubled sea, but in the garden, it was time to watch and pray. Jesus' eyes were so much on the Father, He could not be distracted by a spirit of slumber. Jesus laid awake all night to pray. He is coming to you and me to help us stay alert so that we can watch with Him until He comes as a bridegroom.

Pray this today: Lord Jesus, I want to be a walking prayer meeting, a house of prayer on the earth. Fill my soul with glory and peace so that I can be consumed each moment of my day with you. Teach me to pray. Teach me what continual prayer would look like. Have your way in my heart today as you transform me into a holy sanctuary, filled with your glory. Amen.

18

WATCHMEN ON
THE HILLTOP

*The Amalekites came and attacked the Israelites at Rephidim.
Moses said to Joshua, "Choose some of our men and go out
to fight the Amalekites. Tomorrow I will stand on top of the
hill with the staff of God in my hands." So Joshua fought the
Amalekites as Moses had ordered, and Moses, Aaron and
Hur went to the top of the hill. As long as Moses held up his
hands, the Israelites were winning, but whenever he lowered
his hands, the Amalekites were winning. When Moses' hands
grew tired, they took a stone and put it under him and he sat
on it. Aaron and Hur held his hands up—one on one side, one
on the other—so that his hands remained steady till sunset.
So Joshua overcame the Amalekite army with the sword. Then
the LORD said to Moses, "Write this on a scroll as something to
be remembered and make sure that Joshua hears it, because I
will completely blot out the name of Amalek from under heaven."
Moses built an altar and called it The LORD is my Banner.*

He said, "Because hands were lifted up against the throne of the Lord, the Lord will be at war against the Amalekites from generation to generation."

EXODUS 17:8–16 NIV

In this passage of Scripture, we find the story of Joshua fighting in the valley and Moses praying on the hilltop. As Joshua was going head-to-head with the Amalekites, Moses was holding a rod over the battle with his arms held high. As watchmen-priests, Aaron and Hur came to hold up Moses' hands when he grew weary. And as long as Moses' hands were lifted up high, holding the rod, Joshua would win down in the valley.

The battle was both physical and spiritual. Joshua had to fight the physical battle with his troops in tactical deployment while Moses had to fight the spiritual battle. Moses prayed strategic prayers as he watched from the high place. The rod of God was the assurance to the troops fighting below that God's purpose would stand. God was watching over His armies through Moses, Aaron, and Hur. Everyone's role in this battle was significant and crucial for ultimate victory.

Today we must cover our spiritual leaders with strategic prayer. It's dangerous in this day to be a leader without a team of faithful "armor-bearers" (intercessors) surrounding them. Intercession protects them and keeps their sword sharpened.

There are some in the body of Christ who are called specifically to take a strategic position as personal intercessors for leaders in the church. We could call them the "Aaron and Hur Holding Company." They hold up the arms of the captains in battle. They're called alongside leaders to bless, encourage, uplift, and intercede. May this be the day of your commissioning! May the

Mighty Captain of the Host give you the intercessory assignment to become like an Aaron or Hur of today!

BUILDING A PRAYER WALL

Every prayer, every groan, every cry is a part of hedge-making and wall-building so that others may stand against the enemy. We are to pray and work for the rebuilding of the moral and spiritual walls of protection around peoples and nations (Isaiah 57:14). Intercessors are the Ezras and Nehemiahs of today that are taking a bold stand for righteousness.

With God's authority, our intercession takes a firm stance against the enemy and commands him to vacate strongholds and hiding places he has deceitfully entered. We have the authority to bind and loose by our prayers. Intercessors can crush the enemy's schemes before they are ever unleashed. Look out, devil! Here come God's end-time intercessors! With a militant, reckless abandonment they will stand for the Lord and for the lost! Are you ready to get radical for prayer?

Intercessors must remind the Lord of His promises around the clock—never holding our peace until He establishes His righteousness on earth (Isaiah 62:6–7). We must know God's agenda and, like His secretary, remind Him of His appointments. Our prayers become a wall to keep out demonic hindrances. If ever our nation needed intercessors, it's now. The future belongs to the intercessors. It's time to pray!

Isaiah 21:6–12 provides an interesting understanding of the "watchman ministry" of an intercessor. The Lord instructs Isaiah to post lookouts or watchmen who will be fully alert and at their post night and day: "Go, post a sentry and have him report what he sees! Let him be alert, extremely alert!" Intercessors have strategic assignments given to them by God to scour the spiritual horizons like air traffic controllers. In prayer, God will expose the strategies of the darkness and show the enemy's cards that he intends to play (Jeremiah 51:12).

Listen to what was asked of Isaiah, the prophetic seer, in 21:11: "Watchman, how much longer is the night?" People are looking to those who spend time with God to know what is ahead. The people are longing to know. Who has the heart of God for what is coming? They're asking, "Is the enemy near? Is there danger out there coming our way? When will this be over?" The church is crying out for the night to end and the dawning of the true day to come forth.

The honest reply of the watchman is given in verse 12: "Morning comes, but night endures." The morning of new opportunity is coming to the earth. Yet a night of calamity is also coming. The counsel of the watchman is that this is no time for trifling or playing games with God. If you're going to pray, you better pray. "If you would ask, then come back and ask" (Isaiah 21:12). If you've ever said, "One day I will be a man/woman of prayer," then this is the day to take up that calling!

The Watch of the Lord

The watch of the Lord is one of the ancient tools God is restoring to the church. It's a powerful strategy of intercession that will unleash fresh power to the earth. This is an overlooked model of prayer. Matthew 26:41 says, "Keep alert and pray that you'll be spared from this time of testing. You should have learned by now that your spirit is eager enough, but your humanity is weak." The watch is a military term used to define segments of time during which sentries guard their city from harm, alerting the citizens of approaching enemies. These guards would remain on their watch until it was completed and another gatekeeper would come and take their place (Isaiah 21:6–9).

The night would usually be divided into four watches of three hours each. Mark's Gospel speaks of the "fourth watch of the night" (Mark 6:48). Jesus still comes to His people in the watches of the night. But where are those who are looking to hear from Him? Are there sentries on duty in our city watching over our churches and the needs of others? Let us put out the welcome mat for the Holy Spirit to invade our cities. We need to be possessed for prayer (Lamentations 2:18–19).

The Greek word for *watch* means "to be vigilant, alert." This is our responsibility in prayer: to be vigilant and alert. Eleven times in the Gospels, we are told to watch and be alert! Paul also tells us to "be faithful to pray as intercessors wo are fully alert and giving thanks to God" (Colossians 4:2). It is time to restore the watch of the Lord. Intercessory watchmen must arise and take their place on the walls of our cities. As we stay awake all night long, the enemy will not find an entrance. If there is but one on duty, we can catch him red-handed!

THE WATCHES IN SCRIPTURE

- The morning watch, which includes warfare—Exodus 14:24
- Watching over the city all night—Psalm 101:8
- Waiting and watching for a visitation—Psalm 130:5–6
- Specific hours of prayer in the early church—Acts 3:1
- Morning, afternoon, and evening prayer—Psalm 55:17

- Give Him no rest—Isaiah 62:6–7

- Cry out day and night—Luke 18:1–7

- Watch and record the vision—Habakkuk 2:1–3

- Watching, listening, and waiting on the Lord—Proverbs 8:34–35

- Staying alert and praying at all times—Ephesians 6:18

- Watch with a sober Spirit—1 Peter 4:7

- Be alert, resist the devil, and stand firm—1 Peter 5:8–9

- Wake up and bring life out of death—Revelation 3:2

- We are tempted, but prayer is a key to escape—Matthew 26:41

- Watching in prayer clothes us with power—Revelation 16:15

- Watching in prayer for the Bridegroom—Matthew 24:42–44

- The prayer-chain that binds up the serpent—Revelation 20:1–3

RESURRECTION POWER RELEASED THROUGH OUR PRAYERS

The reality God has planned will always manifest itself first in the prayer life of His intercessors. When you hear from God and then pray His Word, you're impacting the unformed essence of life with the Spirit of God Himself! Thus, God calls us not only to know His Word, but also to pray it. We must go from intellec-tualizing God's Word to being impregnated by it. For everything good and holy that we see manifested in people, churches, and life is first conceived and then birthed in the womb of prayer. As you look around you, you will begin to see answers to prayer being birthed everywhere.

Pray this today: God, I'm overwhelmed by your love for me. Your grace has brought me to a place of intimacy with you. I give myself to you. I accept every prayer assignment you have given me as a joyous way to see you work in answer to my prayers. You are awesome, God! Amen.

19

WE HAVE DUAL CITIZENSHIP

*But we are a colony of heaven on earth as we cling tightly to
our life-giver, the Lord Jesus Christ, who will transform our
humble bodies and transfigure us into the identical likeness of
his glorified body. And using his matchless power, he continually
subdues everything to himself.*

PHILIPPIANS 3:20–21

God is talking to His church in this moment of human history not only to realize *who* we are in Christ, but to understand *where* we are in Christ. We are dual citizens of both earth and heaven. As you begin to pray from a throne room perspective, ask Him how He wants you to pray in this time of epic change. As you survey the earth from His perspective, it will forever change how you pray—bringing heaven's perspective to your prayers.

Have you ever wondered why the devil hates intercessors? Simply stated, it's because you are a threat to his dark kingdom! Intercessors come under unusual attack from demonic powers because they are the ones doing some of the greatest damage to his strategies, schemes, and web of deceit. As an enthroned intercessor, you make the devil jealous.

Isaiah 14:12–17 has an account of one called the "morning star or son of the dawn." He had been cast down to the earth for his pride and rebellion. Scholars conclude this is a clear reference to Lucifer, the devil. Listen to what caused his fall:

You said in your heart, "I will ascend into heaven and set my throne above the stars of God. I will rule on the mountain of the congregation, on the highest place of the sacred mountain. I will rise past the tops of the clouds and rival the Most High God!"

- He boasted that he would ascend, but you have already been seated on high!

- He boasted that his throne would be above the stars of God—you are invited to sit on Jesus' throne!

- He boasted that he would be on the sacred mountain—you are seated on Mt. Zion!

- He boasted that he would rise past the clouds—you are seated in the glory cloud!

- He boasted that he would rival the Most High—you are destined to be like Christ!

This is why the devil hates you—you have fulfilled his dreams! You've been freely given the place he's sought after. It cost you nothing, for it was grace that has lifted you on high. He's been cast down, but you've been freely and fully anointed with the Spirit of God and raised to sit with Christ in the high places. Since he can't touch God, he will come after you with jealous fury. Does that explain why sometimes it's such a struggle for you to break through in prayer? But remember that you're covered in the blood of the Lamb. Hidden in the high places, the devil can't even find you (Colossians 3:1–4).

THE JESUS STAIRWAY AND HIS ASCENDING ANGELS

There are at least two clear references to the "Jesus Stairway" in the Bible. The first is found in Genesis 28. Jacob was running away from his angry brother Esau. After having walked for two or three days, he was weary and exhausted when night fell. At twilight, he set up camp at Bethel. Some believe this was the ancient place where his grandfather, Abraham, erected an altar to Yahweh years before (Genesis 12:8).

In his helpless, lonely condition, Jacob would be given a new revelation. With stones for a pillow, heaven as a canopy above, and the cold ground beneath, Jacob falls asleep and dreams. In his dream he has a vision of the Almighty, and he hears the words of God. Then Jacob sees a stairway, a ladder reaching up to heaven. Upon this ladder, he sees angels ascending and descending. God Himself was at the top of this angel-filled stairway speaking to him. What a mysterious sight this must have been to the frightened Jacob!

The second place we find a clear reference to this stairway to heaven is in the New Testament—in John 1. Jesus Christ is clearly the ladder that reaches from earth (His human nature) to heaven (His heavenly nature). Jesus spoke to Nathaniel using the same terminology, saying, "I prophesy to you eternal truth: From now on you will see an open heaven and gaze upon the Son of Man like a stairway reaching into the sky with the messengers of God climbing up and down upon Him!" (John 1:51). Jacob received the glorious revelation that Jesus is the stairway to heaven!

Jesus is the only valid entry into the spirit realm. He's the way into the heavenly realms. This Jesus-ladder was filled with angels ascending and descending. But who are these angels?

Note the order. These angels ascended first. It doesn't say they were descending and ascending, which would be true if they were the angels of heaven. If you ascend first, you are leaving earth to go to heaven. Whoever these angels are, they ascend from the earth to heaven and then descend back to the earth.

These "angels" are intercessors! There are angels that are the angels of heaven and then there are angels that are human. The Greek word used in the New Testament for angels is merely *angelos* or "messengers." This can refer to people or to heavenly angels. Paul wrote to the Galatians and told them they had welcomed him in their midst as if he were an angel of God (Galatians 4:14). In Revelation 2–3, John is instructed to write to the seven churches and to the seven angels of those churches. Those angels were messengers or pastors over those churches. In Strong's Concordance, the word there means "pastor." In the Old Testament, even Jesus, in His pre-incarnate form, appeared as the "angel of the Lord." In Genesis 18:2, three angels come to Abraham and are described as "three men" (compare Genesis 19:1). Angels are also seen as the end-time reapers in Matthew 24:31. God's angels, His messengers, will be sent as fiery flames of revival into all the earth. From the ministry of angels (messengers), the great harvest will be brought in.

Beloved, you and I are the angels that ascend and descend upon the Son of Man, the Jesus-ladder! We're the ascending angels. The enthroned intercessors are those who go up through the open door (Revelation 4:1) and come down with authority to execute the will of God on the earth.

This revelation given to Jacob was repeated by the Lord to Nathaniel. Nathaniel had his eyes on the earth when he said, "What good thing could ever come from Nazareth?" but Jesus told him his eyes would see an open heaven. Jesus was prophesying of an end-time open heaven that would allow access to the messengers of the Lord (intercessors) to go into the throne room by the blood of the Lamb and return with the strategies, wisdom, and glory of heaven. The Lord wants you, His enthroned intercessor, to climb the Jesus-ladder and release on earth what God has released in heaven!

Listen to the words of St. Germanus of Constantinople as he speaks of "climbing this ladder":

> The souls of Christians are called to assemble with the prophets, apostles, and hierarchies in order to recline with Abraham, Isaac, and Jacob at the mystical banquet of the Kingdom of Christ. Thereby having come into the unity of faith and communion of the Spirit through the dispensation of the One who died for us and is sitting at the right hand of the Father, we are no longer on earth but standing by the royal throne of God in heaven, where Christ is, just as He Himself says: "Righteous Father, sanctify in Your name those whom You have given me, so that where I am, they may be with Me."[3]

---

[3] St. Germanus of Constantinople, *On the Divine Liturgy*, trans. Paul Meyendorff (Crestwood, NY: St. Vladimir's Seminary Press, 1984), 101.

In the *Odes of Solomon,* there are frequent references to ecstatic, visionary trips to paradise.[4] One example states, "I rested on the Spirit of the Lord, and She [the Holy Spirit] lifted me up to heaven." End-time intercession must become an act of climbing the Jesus-ladder. We go up to the heavens with our cries for intervention. Then we descend back to earth with the answer! Intercession is seeing heaven open and the messengers of God ascending and descending upon the Son of Man. It's time to go up, holy angels! It is time to let your heart-cry ascend until the promise descends. We all have access because we are united to Him (Ephesians 2:18). His door is open, and the stairway is available to you and to me.

The answers you need are not on the earth, but they are in the throne room. And the throne room is closer than you think. This is the ascending highway spoken of by the prophet Isaiah (Isaiah 35:8–9; 57:14–15; 62:10). Climb that Jesus-ladder and find the fulfillment of your covenant promises, just like Jacob did. Answers to prayer will be found when we ascend with our requests and return in faith with the promise fulfilled. Time to go up the "secret stairway": the hiding place on the mountainside of the Lord (Song of Songs 2:14).

What would God tell Jacob at the top of this ladder? He reveals Himself to Jacob as the One who will never leave or forsake Him. A revelation of grace and a stream of assurances washes over wayward Jacob! And God speaks His affirmation and renews His blessing to all the ascending ones in these last days.

Be bold, you angel! Go up the Jesus-ladder into that place where He has already seated you as an intercessor, a bride at His

---

[4] David E. Aune, *Prophecy in Early Christianity and the Ancient Mediterranean World* (Grand Rapids: Wm. B. Eerdmans, 1991), 287.

side! Enthroned intercessors will be those "violent ones" who take the kingdom by force. With the anointing and zeal of John the Baptist, you won't be held back by those who tell them what they can't do. Go up, you mighty champions, you angels of the Lord, until you become the "voice of the Lord" to the nations of the earth!

Pray this today: Lord, you have given me access into the glory and throne room of heaven. I am so thankful that my prayers rise before you as incense. I long to be a voice, an outlet of your glory streaming into the earth. Let it be so! Amen.

20

THE THRONE ROOM

Then suddenly ... I saw a portal open into the heavenly realm,
and the same trumpet-voice I heard speaking with me at the
beginning said, "Ascend into this realm!"

REVELATION 4:1

By the grace of God, every barrier between you and heaven has been removed. Sacred blood has been spilled for you, ensuring that you can come freely, without hesitation, before Father-God! What a miracle is this! You look like Jesus when you come before Him, for the nature of the Lamb is now within you. God has now seated you at His right hand, the place of favor and authority. You are robed, crowned, and enthroned. It doesn't get much better than that!

Many of God's prophets had throne room encounters. These will increase as we get closer to the unveiling of Christ. Isaiah saw the Lord God high and lifted up. He was taken into the throne room and saw nothing but fire and glory. Ezekiel had the throne room come to him! It was like a chariot-throne surrounded by blazing fire, wings, wheels, and eyes. Daniel saw the chariot-throne with fire coming out from before Him. Amos, Zechariah, and other prophetic seers had encounters in the throne zone.

And this is where Christ now invites us to come. Boldly, with confidence in the blood of Jesus, and draw near! He is saying to us what He said to John on Patmos in Revelation 4:1. It's as though He is saying to us, "Rise up into this heavenly realm, and enter the throne room so that I can unveil Myself to you!"

This is a call to "come up higher" to the third heaven! John has just entered into another realm through this "door standing open in heaven." His environment has entirely changed, and I believe *his focus has changed.* His focus for two chapters (Revelation 2–3) was with sin and the church in the earth, but now his focus is upon the Throne of God and the Glory of God. The Throne and the Glory now operate on earth through *us!*

This *door opened in heaven* speaks of an entrance granted into a realm beyond the flesh, beyond the physical and psychical senses, into the realm of the Spirit. That is where John entered, and that is the character of the things John saw. He beheld heavenly things—spiritual realities. He saw a throne set in heaven—he perceived the authority, power, and dominion of the Spirit. He saw living creatures in the throne, the principle of manifest life in the Spirit. He saw the four living creatures in the midst of the throne and twenty-four elders round about the throne—the King-Priest ministry after the order of Melchizedek in the power of an endless life. There will be a vast number of people that hear the voice of the Lord in this hour. They will see that a door has been opened in the heavenly realm through which those who are obedient shall enter into a state of being and a ministry of unsurpassed and unimaginable glory—in the throne zone!

WHAT IS THIS DOOR?

Jesus Himself has told us! Of all that Jesus said about the life of sonship and entrance into the glory and power of the kingdom of God, nothing is more significant than these words: "I am the door—the gateway into the eternal realm." He alone is *the new and living way*, the truth, and the life. What a strange but wonderful figure of speech—Jesus, the door! Now what does a door signify? One can judge the interior of a house by its door. Is the door shabby, with its paint peeling off, hanging on a single hinge? Then it opens into a house of the same character—run down, in disorder, unkempt. If, on the other hand, the door is spacious, costly, ornamental, and distinctive, one has a right to expect that the building into which it leads is splendid, spacious, and beautiful.

Truly, this metaphor of Christ as the door is enchanting! He is the door to the life of sonship, the life of immortality, the life of glory and power. And if he is but the door, what must the full experience of that life be like? It cannot be less than Christ! It must be as much as Jesus was to His disciples and the multitudes who followed Him—that much and more!

To the Lord Jesus Himself, *the heavens were opened* at His baptism, and He saw the Spirit of God descending like a dove, and lighting upon Him, and a voice from heaven saying, "This is the Son I love, and my greatest delight is in him" (Matthew 3:16–17). This opening of the heavens to Christ was His public introduction as the Son of God! The opened heavens declared His sonship! It marks the beginning of that full revelation through Him of the mystery of God revealed in sons! Have you heard the voice saying to you, *Come up into a heavenly realm?* All who are called to be a prayer partner with Jesus have heard that voice!

When we read these meaningful words of a door opened in heaven, with our mind's eye we can visualize a huge door creaking on its hinges, opening up in the sky. But that is not at all what John saw! The Greek word for door is *thura,* meaning "a portal" or "an entrance." A portal or an entrance is opened unto us! The word can also mean "a vestibule," and it denotes the first awareness of entrance into something. It is the place of transition from the earthly to the heavenly. The Greek text indicates that the door is there and it's *standing open.* This portal is the invitation of the Father by the Spirit, for upon seeing the door, John immediately *"became* in the Spirit" or passed through the door and found Himself standing in the throne room. A portal is a passage into another realm. The door is the spirit of Christ, and the spirit of His sonship is the open gateway into the throne room of the heavens!

"Instantly I was taken into the spirit realm, and behold—I saw a heavenly throne set in place and someone seated upon it" (Revelation 4:2). When the eagle-eyed seer of Patmos, being in the Spirit, looked aloft into the heavens, *he saw a throne.* This throne represents dominion, authority, and power. We have to rise into a new realm to really understand the government of God: His throne! Everything centers on the throne. The first and last thing that will be seen in the open heavens is the throne, with the Lamb in the center!

As we ascend in the Spirit to reign with Christ in His throne, it indicates a departure from the candlestick in the Holy Place to follow our glorious and exalted forerunner beyond the veil into the throne room of the Holiest of All. It means entrance into a greater, deeper, and higher relationship with Christ the Lord.

HIS THRONE IS THE MERCY SEAT

As John moves through the veil, he sees the throne room with One sitting on the throne. This throne is actually the *blood-sprinkled mercy seat*! This is where we are invited to sit (Revelation 3:21) and fellowship with Jesus! Thank God, the throne of the universe is the throne of mercy! All men may boldly approach the throne of grace. When Jesus says, "Come unto me," He is not speaking geographically; He is speaking experientially! The journey to Christ and into Christ is not outward or physical; it is inward and spiritual.

At the conclusion of the messages to the churches in Revelation, the Lord says, "Behold, I stand at the door and knock." Notice that Jesus does not call this "a door" or "your door" or identify it as any particular door. He calls it *the* door. It is one specific door, the identity of which is taken for granted. It is abundantly clear that the door He knocks upon is *the door* that separates the realm of the seven lampstands and the throne room! This door is the same as the veil that separates the Holy Place from the Most Holy Place!

First, the Lord stands knocking at the door. He follows this with the promise of raising us up to His throne to overcome all things. Then, only two verses later, John says, "After this I looked, and saw a portal open in heaven." And through that door, he saw the throne! Do you not see the mystery? It seems clear that the "door" that was opened in heaven was the very same "door" that Jesus knocked upon. It is the gateway between the two realms, the gateway between the lampstand realm and the throne!

Christ comes into us from the heavenly realm to feast with us. This means He *descends* through *the door*, but we must open it! What a table He has spread as He has taught us of Himself, His word, His ways, and His will. In the holy intimacy of this supping together, He has brought us to a fuller and more complete knowing and experiencing of who He is! And because we have opened the door … the door is now still *standing open into the heavenly realm!* Christ came through the door to feast with us, and now He arises from the meal, He bids us go through the door and enter with Him into His throne!

The realm of heaven is calling you to arise and come up higher. The mountains of spice are waiting for you to visit. The Throne Zone is the place of prayer with Jesus on the Sea of Glass. This is the same message Jesus speaks to every one of His lovers, for we are His beloved.

> Arise, my dearest. Hurry, my darling.
> Come away with me!
> I have come as you have asked
> to draw you to my heart and lead you out.
> For now is the time, my beautiful one.
> The season has changed,
> the bondage of your barren winter has ended,
> and the season of hiding is over and gone.
> The rains have soaked the earth
> and left it bright with blossoming flowers.
> The season for singing and pruning the vines has arrived.
> I hear the cooing of doves in our land, filling the air with
> songs to awaken you and guide you forth.
> Can you not discern this new day of destiny breaking forth
> around you?
> The early signs of my purposes and plans are bursting forth.
> The budding vines of new life are now blooming everywhere.
> The fragrance of their flowers whispers,
> "There is change in the air."

Arise, my love, my beautiful companion,
and run with me to the higher place.
For now is the time to arise and come away with me.
(Song of Songs 2:10–13)

Pray this today: Jesus, I hear your voice calling me to pray. I will arise now in search of you. I will find you and not let you go until I am fully one with you. I will be your prayer partner and rise to run away with you! Amen.

21

THE ONE WHO SITS ON THE THRONE

*I saw a heavenly throne being set in place
and Someone seated upon it.*

REVELATION 4:2

As John went into the heavenly realm, he saw the One who was enthroned. He had no form, only radiance! John stood in the very reality of heaven as he was caught up in the highest realm of the Spirit. The One he saw was Spirit (John 4:23–24). Here seated in the splendor of the omnipresent heavenly-spiritual realm, John gazed upon the One of many colors. Even though He did not have a natural form, John could see Him in and by the Spirit.

John witnessed firsthand the throne of Almighty God being set in place with Someone being enthroned. This beautiful throne is established with power, security, and governmental authority over all. There is one seated there, for the work has been completed. The One seated on the throne means the Lamb finished the work and sat down! All that was necessary to purify a last-days people has been completed! And here is what excites me: we are invited to sit with him as overcomers on his throne (Revelation 3:21)!

This is not the throne of God in its eternalness, but a new, fresh, and more glorious revelation of the throne in an advanced manifestation. For John sees it not as something that had long since been settled in the heavenly realm, but just as it was—taking up its rest in this place. It was while John was witnessing what is taking place in the heavenly realm that the throne was being set in place! That is the sense of the Greek text. The expression is in a tense which denotes unfinished action, reaching its completion at the time of the seeing.

Perhaps we can view the throne as a developing throne, just as every purpose of God is unfolding in a progressive manner from age to age. Isn't the body of Christ growing and maturing, being built up as a spiritual temple? And isn't the bride of Christ being prepared and making herself ready for the marriage union? Even the kingdom of God is expanding, for of the increase of His government and authority, there will be no end.

Heaven—a Dimension of Life

The Greek word for heaven, *ouranos*, appears in the New Testament 275 times. The meaning of the word is "elevation, height, exaltation, eminence." Therefore, we have exactly the same thought if we say, "My throne is elevation, height, exaltation, and eminence." That, my beloved, is the central idea of heaven in the New Testament! *Ouranos* is more than a location beyond the blue. It is the height, the very pinnacle of glory, eminence, exaltation, majesty, authority, and power over all God's limitless domain. This authority is in and by the Spirit, for God is Spirit and does not sit upon a physical throne.

The heavenly realm can be seen, but not as a planet somewhere out in the vastness of infinity—it is a sphere or a realm of spiritual, divine reality. It is a dimension of life. It is the invisible realm of Spirit that transcends this gross material realm. It is as omnipresent as God is omnipresent. Christ has ascended to the highest heaven and therefore has been given all power and all authority in the heavens and earth! And this very Christ is now the door—the "star gate" into the throne zone! The door is standing open, dear one, and a mighty voice is inviting you to come into the throne zone! What a wonderful realm is waiting for us!

THE OMNIPRESENT THRONE

Throne Room Prayer doesn't mean you have to go anywhere to come up to the throne realm! It is closer to you than the air you breathe. It's closer to you even than the blood that courses through your veins. In the power of the kingdom of God within you, there is no limitation at all. In fact, the throne room is now found in Christ within us! Your spirit, made holy by blood and grace, is now the throne room where Christ is King and Lord of your life. Throne Room Prayer is praying in the dimension of our spirit being, discovering that the portal has been opened and we enter into the heavenly realm whenever we want. We draw near to God in faith, not by sight. We draw from the wealth and power of Christ within us. In the throne zone, you can see all things as they really are!

If God is omnipresent, then His throne is the omnipresent throne. And we cannot limit the God who fills the heavens to a chair-like throne that we have here on earth. You cannot make the glory of God squeeze into a chair and sit there. Heaven is His throne (Isaiah 66:1; Acts 7:29). The dwelling place of God cannot be any smaller or more limited than He is! The whole vast realm of the heavens is His throne. The heavens are His throne, which means that He rules and reigns in the realm of the Spirit and by His Spirit. If we could measure the extent of the Spirit, from one end of the heavens to the other, we would then be able to estimate the extent of His throne.

He doesn't live in buildings made with hands, and He doesn't sit on a chair made with hands. We must view God not as a limited physical being that can sit on a tangible throne in one restricted locality somewhere out beyond the blue. God is spirit, heaven is His throne, and He is everywhere present. This means His throne is a spiritual throne and is everywhere. This should simplify for you what Throne Room Prayer is all about—coming into the higher realm of the Spirit and bringing our prayers before Him. Heaven, therefore, is not far away! God is everywhere, and His throne is everywhere, for His throne is a powerful symbol of His omnipotent power, authority, and sovereignty. There is no need to go anywhere physically to relate to God's throne. The journey is a spiritual one! The throne is all around you, within you, and present equally everywhere within the realm of spirit in which God exists and dwells. You can either experience or ascend that throne within yourself through union with Christ and the release of His power.

In Revelation, the word *throne* is found thirty times; in chapter 4 alone, it appears twelve times. Twelve is the divine number of governmental authority. There is One who is seated on the throne, ruling and reigning over the universe. It is so important to our prayer life to know that God is in charge, and He rules from the heavenly realm. Yet He also calls us into that throne room experience to encounter His authority and to release it on earth. We are called to reign as king-priests on this planet.

The Hebrew word translated "reign" is *malak*, and it means "to reign, to ascend the throne, to induct into royalty." Thus, when we are called to "Come up hither" to share His throne, we are called to ascend the throne and to be inducted into the royal power of that throne! Therefore, as the elect hear His voice and hasten to His call, we are ascending the very throne of Christ in a greater relationship with Him and in Him. We are being *inducted* into the royalty of the throne of Christ—into His *reigning realm*! We are enthroned, robed, and crowned!

"His appearance was sparkling like crystal (jasper) and glowing like a carnelian (sardius) gemstone. Surrounding the throne was a circle of green light, like an emerald rainbow" (Revelation 4:3). He had no form, only radiance! John was not looking into the natural elements when he saw the One on the throne. John stood in the very reality of heaven as he was caught up in the highest realm of the Spirit. The One John saw is spirit (John 4:23–24). What John saw was colors and light, for God is *light*. The crystal, diamond-like glory of God was mingled with the red glow and the emerald rainbow. John saw the Being of God as light streaming and pulsating from the throne room. This is the God you come to when you pray with Jesus on the Sea of Glass.

JASPER (CRYSTAL)

Jasper was the last of the gems (the third stone in the fourth row) in the high priest's breastplate (Exodus 28:20), and it was likely the diamond. The jasper-diamond splendor, the sparkling radiance of His being, diffuses light everywhere. A diamond is precious—everyone wants one—and is hard and unbreakable—and so is the throne of God! This radiant diamond-like stone is what the Father looked like to John when he saw this glorious light emanating out of the Father.

SARDIUS

This a blood-red gemstone, and it was the first stone in the first row of the breastplate of Aaron, the high priest (Exodus 28:17). The sardius (carnelian, ruby) can be compared to God's throbbing heart of fiery passion, burning as a garment. What an amazing truth we discover in the throne room! Our High Priest, the One who is the First and the Last, the Beginning and the Ending (Revelation 1:8), has the appearance of the first and last stones of the breastplate. Here is glory indescribable! The scene is one of luminous splendor!

"SURROUNDING THE THRONE WAS A CIRCLE OF GREEN LIGHT, LIKE AN EMERALD RAINBOW"

There is this emerald rainbow arching over His throne, which, of course, speaks of the mercy of God. All that God does from His throne is covered with mercy. This was not a typical rainbow, for a rainbow has seven colors. This was more like a halo of light, shining all around the throne. It was a full circle, not a half-circle. It could have been horizontally or vertically around the throne. The Greek also allows for the translation "a rainbow made of emerald."

The emerald rainbow points to God's mercy and covenant love, for He gave the sign of a rainbow to Noah, signifying that He would never again destroy the world through a flood. The rainbow around the throne would be a clear symbol that everything

God does (coming from His throne of majesty) is surrounded with grace and mercy. The Hebrew word for "emerald" is *bareqeth*, which can also be translated "flashing of light" (Exodus 28:17). God's glory is represented by these three stones: jasper, carnelian, and emerald.

When you come before God in prayer, you come to the emerald-rainbow promise of mercy waiting for you! We come before the throne of grace and mercy as sons and daughters, beloved of the Father. Our prayers must always be rooted and grounded in this revelation of mercy. The green hue of this rainbow points to *life*, not judgment. The rainbow given as a sign to Noah is a promise of life. The rainbow in the throne room of God is that same promise of mercy and life given to the lovers of God.

Mercy is waiting for you in the throne zone. Come and take your place, mighty sons and daughters of the Most High God. He is waiting to give you life abundant, mercy overflowing, and grace indescribable!

Pray this today: Father of mercy, God of all grace, I come before you in the heavenly realm. I am your loving child, one in whom you delight. I find my true rest when I come before you. Take away the fear that would keep me distant from you. Wash over me again with your life and mercy. I draw near to you to tell you how much I love you. Draw me over and over again into your cloud-filled chamber room of glory, until I never want to leave. In your holy name. Amen.

22

THE TWENTY-FOUR ELDERS

Encircling the great throne were twenty-four thrones with elders in glistening white garments seated upon them, each wearing a golden crown of victory.

REVELATION 4:4

There is more than one throne in the glorious heavenly realm. As John is taken in the spirit, he sees a circle of thrones around the throne of God. These twenty-four thrones were for the elders that gather in worship. Like the tribes of Israel gathered around the Tabernacle, we see these elders gathered around the throne of glory. Who are these twenty-four elders, and what do their twenty-four thrones symbolize?

Some scholars surmise that they are angelic beings serving as God's cabinet officers. But this is very unlikely because we see the elders singing in Revelation 5 that they have been redeemed by the blood of the Lamb, and no angel experiences redemption—we do!

Others see the twenty-four elders representing the twenty-four books of the prophets included in our Bibles. Still others see the elders as a metaphor of the twenty-four hours of the day, making them an indication that worship is non-stop in the heavenly realm. Although these pictures may have some reality, the clear truth of the twenty-four elders is that they represent men and women from the nations of the earth, both Jew and Gentile, who have been redeemed. The New Testament speaks of us as "one new man" from both Jews (who had twelve tribes) and the church (who had twelve chosen apostles).

Look carefully at what this verse says about these elders:

- The twenty-four elders each sat on a throne and were reigning with Christ. He has made us kings and queens to rule and reign—*enthroned* with Him. Men and women who believe are enthroned with the Godhead! Mystery of mysteries! God shares His throne room with His people!

- They are *robed* in white garments, a picture of Christ's righteousness. These are the robes of a priest—and He has made us priests (Leviticus 6:10; 16:4). The priestly role includes worshipping, interceding, and communicating God's heart to others. We are God's priests who best represent God forever and who mediate His glory to others in the age to come. God's humility shines brightly in choosing us to represent Him. White is the color of purity or holiness. Bright and clean linen was given to those who persevere or overcome (Revelation 3:4–5, 18; 6:11; 7:9, 13; 15:6; 19:8, 14).

- They have crowns. He has *crowned* us with glory and honor. The elders wear gold crowns. There are two Greek words describing two different types of crowns in the New Testament. One is the crown of a ruler (*diadem*), the other was the crown of a victor (*stephanos*) who won a race in the Greek athletic games. The Greek word for crown in Revelation 4:4 is *stephanos*, which speaks of a victor's crown rather than a king's diadem. It is the golden crown of the overcomer who has fought the "beast life" and has won by the blood of the Lamb.

We are *enthroned, robed,* and *crowned*—all because of what Jesus has done. The twenty-four elders (a metaphor for the over-comers) were rewarded for gaining significant victories over sin in their life. The angels are not rewarded for victory over sin, but they are judged if they do sin. Crowns in Revelation are given for endurance or perseverance and are only promised to victors or overcomers (Revelation 2:10; 3:11). These crowns of victory imply faithfulness and endurance. When you come before God in prayer, remember what He has done for you. You are enthroned, robed in white, and given a crown.[5]

The twenty-four elders in their glistening white robes are priests around the throne. They intercede, worship, move God's heart, and share His authority. They are the royal, enthroned priesthood seated before God to be co-rulers in eternity. In 1 Chronicles 24:19, we learn that king David divided the Levitical priesthood into twenty-four groups who would take turns serving God in His earthly Tabernacle. These twenty-four groups were

---

[5] For an online, in-depth study of the throne room, visit www.tptbible-school.com/courses.

under the headship of twenty-four elders! The picture we see in the throne room is the realm of priests who reign with Christ seated upon thrones. Reigning priests!

"And pulsing from the throne were blinding flashes of lightning, crashes of thunder, and voices. And burning before the throne are seven blazing torches, which represent the seven Spirits of God" (Revelation 4:5). Amazing! When you enter the throne zone, you will see lightning flashes bringing greater glory and the sounds of thunder crashing over the worshippers. And you will hear voices like a waterfall speaking their praises to Almighty God. What do all these sights and sounds represent? These manifestations are meant to reveal more of Christ within us!

- Flashes of lightning represent the destructive power of God to destroy the enemy. After Jesus sent out the Seventy, they returned, and Jesus told them, "I watched Satan topple until he fell suddenly from heaven like lightning" (Luke 10:18). And in Matthew 24:27, we see Christ's appearing as lightning from the east—the door of the Temple!

- The rumble of thunder is the deep yearnings within God's heart to reveal Christ and thunder out His glory through us, the ones who share this throne!

- The voices are the voices of God's lovers, the worshippers in heaven, the corporate appearing of the sons of God in manifestation. Those with Christ formed in them become a voice to the world. In Exodus 20:18–19, the same manifestations of lightning and thunder appear from Mount Sinai, but the people would not endure it and told Moses, "Let not God speak with us, lest we die."

But in Revelation 4, God's people have heard with ears opened and now become voices at the throne.

THE SEVEN SPIRITS OF GOD

And burning before the throne were seven blazing torches, which represent the seven Spirits of God. (Revelation 4:5)

Seven burning torches before the throne! This points us to the lampstand with its seven branches (Exodus 25:31–37). It was one golden lampstand, yet it had seven lamps with burning oil (Zechariah 4:2). Each branch of the lampstand represents one of the seven Spirits of God. The seven-fold Spirit of God is burning with light, glory, and revelation in the throne zone! This is what you encounter as you join with Jesus to pray with Him on the Sea of Glass!

The lamps of burning fire were igniting the people of God for more revelation. These are the seven manifestations of the Spirit of God. Seven, in the Scriptures, is the most sacred number of the Hebrews. It is the number denoting *spiritual perfection and completeness*. The seven spirits of God, seven denoting spiritual perfection and completeness, are a picture of the fullness of the Spirit of God. These seven lamps of fire represent the seven spirits of sonship (Isaiah 11:1–5). This is the sevenfold sonship anointing that rested and continues to rest upon the firstborn Son of God! This mighty and glorious anointing shall come also upon all the unveiled sons of God in these last days. We will fully rise to become God's kings and priests on earth as it is in heaven!

A CRYSTAL SEA OF GLASS

And in front of the throne there was pavement like a crystal sea of glass. Around the throne and on each side stood four living creatures, full of eyes in front and behind. (Revelation 4:6)

The assembly hall of heaven has a transparent, crystal floor—a sapphire pavement that stretches as far as the eye can see. All the glory of the rainbow and its colors is mirrored in that crystal sea. We find in Revelation 15:2 that the sea is mingled with flaming fire. This is where the billions of the saints and angels come. It's the big conference center before the throne. It is a *Sea* of Glass, not a lake or pond. It is a vast sea of peace and glory. This is where you come when you intercede before the Father of Love.

The wicked are like the raging sea that never rests (Isaiah 57:20–21), but the righteous are gathered on a peaceful sea that is beautiful and calm, still and serene (Psalm 89:9). God parted the Red Sea to let the redeemed pass through in peace. Jesus stilled the waves of the troubled sea when He walked the earth. The peaceful Sea of Glass is in contrast to the turbulent "sea of humanity." Jude also described the natural man when he said, "They are wild waves of the sea, flinging out the foam of their shame and disgrace" (Jude 13).

Heaven has no turmoil, no surging sea—only peace. The Lamb rules from His throne and gathers His lovers on the crystal sea. The Lamb rules over the inner raging of the sea and He stills all its storms! All are quieted by the Lord, the Spirit, who arises from within us giving us peace, confidence, and truth. And then follows the calm. This Sea of Glass represents the transformed believers who have been forever changed, filled with peace, and ruled by the Lamb. There is a beast that comes out of the sea of humanity, but in heaven, there is a peace that is produced by the life-nature of the Lamb.

Reading further in the book of Revelation, we find the

overcomers standing on the Sea of Glass mingled with fire (Revelation 15:2). They have harps and sing the song of Moses and the Lamb—the song of deliverance, the song of the overcomer! They are no longer going through the sea, nor being tossed about by it, but they are standing on top of it. The message is clear—the crystal sea speaks of the nature in which they stand, and their walk has become stable and transparent! The fact that what is underneath their feet is solid, brilliant, and clear reveals to us the great truth that they are rooted and grounded in the pure, perfect, and holy nature of Christ within.

John actually gazed upon this Sea of Glass twice. Both of these descriptions provide symbolical views of both a people and a state of being. Glass is formed from melted sand. Individual grains of sand (people) are melted into one. John beheld this Sea of Glass mingled with fire—having come through the furnace of afflictions. As the Lord says, "See, I have purified you in the furnace of affliction ... I have refined you in the fire" (Isaiah 48:10). In the image and likeness of Christ, they are bonded together in a divine union of life. John sees the whole redeemed company not as millions of individual grains of sand, but as one body, even as a crystal Sea of Glass!

The Sea of Glass also points to the laver, which stood between the bronze altar and the Tabernacle, a place of washing for the priests before they approached God (Exodus 30:18–19). The laver was formed out of the melted bronze mirrors of the people of Israel (Exodus 38:8). The mirror aspect of the laver represents the way that Christ, through His face-to-face relationship with us, shows us our imperfections and then washes them away. This is the laver, the washing place where you prepare to be in the Holy of Holies! The Sea of Glass, the mirror of sapphire, points out what is still lacking and what we need to surrender. As the elders bowed down, they saw themselves in the reflection of the mirror pavement and quickly cast their crowns to the Lamb who is worthy. They saw themselves in the light of the lampstand and gave up the glory to Christ (2 Corinthians 4:6).

When you come before God, you also stand in this glory, washed in love, made ready to present your requests to Him.

Pray this today: Glorious Father, I come before you now in the heavenly realm. You have opened a portal for me to pass through so that I might commune with you. I enter into my calling as an enthroned intercessor, seated at your right hand. I am thankful for the white garment of righteousness and the golden crown of victory on my head. I take my place humbly before you and lay my requests before your throne. Amen.

23

ENTHRONED INTERCESSORS

*He raised us up with Christ the exalted One and we ascended
with him into the glorious perfection and authority of the
heavenly realm, for we are now co-seated as one with Christ.*

EPHESIANS 2:6

It would be impossible for God to give you more than what
you already have in Jesus Christ! Beloved, you are blessed with
everything heaven can give (Ephesians 1:3). And that's not
when you die, but right now! You are as ready for heaven as you
will ever be! Fully justified, fully forgiven … you are God's beloved
child. He likes you! He loves to hear your voice and calls it sweet
(Song of Songs 2:14). You look like Jesus when you come before
the Father. He receives you and loves you just like He receives and
loves His Son (Ephesians 1:6).

How does it feel to be accepted just as you are? Your inheritance as a Christian is to become a look-alike of Jesus Christ. The
Father loves His Son so much that He is determined to fill heaven

with people just like Him! And the Father is working in you every day to make you more like His Son. All of your life is meant to train you for ruling and reigning with Jesus. You are in schooling for ruling and in training for reigning. Your personal destiny is already fixed. You were "destined from the beginning to share the likeness of His Son" (Romans 8:29).

WELCOME TO THE THRONE ROOM

As a beloved child of God, you've been escorted into the throne room of heaven already. Grace has brought you home. As you pray to the Father, you are praying seated in heavenly places in Christ Jesus, seated in His throne room. Read this verse carefully, then read it again. Place it on the tablet of your heart: "He raised us up with Christ, the exalted One, and we ascended with him into the glorious perfection and authority of the heavenly realm, for we are now co-seated as one with Christ!" (Ephesians 2:6).

You are an enthroned intercessor. You have rights and privileges before the Father. Grace has fully gifted you to cry out to the Father of Eternity. If God were to bless you any more and raise you up any higher, it would be a threat to the Trinity! Every privilege that Jesus has you have. The righteousness that Jesus has you have. The position before the Father that Jesus has you have. Got it? It's time to rejoice!

There is a company of people in heaven that have been redeemed by the blood of the Lamb. They're the saints of God. They're you and I. We are enthroned intercessors who gaze on the glory and beauty of Jesus as we speak to Him in prayer. If you will begin to see yourself as already seated with Him in glory, your prayer life will never be the same.

Israel asked God to be an intercessor. Their faith was in His ability to come and rescue them. Listen to their plea: "Awake God, awake! Arm of Yahweh, put on Your robe of strength! Awake and do the works of power as in ancient days" (Isaiah 51:9). But now listen to the Lord's reply: "Wake up! Open your eyes! Beautiful Zion, be clothed with your majestic strength! … Arise and shake off your dust! Rise up and sit enthroned, Jerusalem" (Isaiah 52:1–2). God's answer is that it's time for you to awake and stir yourself. It's time to take off the dust-man and put on the glory-garments. Rise to the place where you belong and sit at His side as we bring forth destiny to the earth! He's calling you to be an enthroned intercessor!

> We have already come near to God in a totally different realm, the Zion-realm, for we have entered the city of the Living God [God's throne room], which is the New Jerusalem in heaven! We have joined to the festal gathering of myriads of angels in their joyous celebration! (Hebrews 12:22)

> And to the one who conquers I will give the privilege of sitting with me on my throne, just as I conquered and sat down with my Father on his throne. (Revelation 3:21)

> Let the beloved of the LORD rest secure in him, for he shields him (her) all day long, and the one the LORD loves rests between his shoulders. (Deuteronomy 33:12 NIV)

God is asking His people to reposition their prayer altars. He's calling His church fully to realize their position in Christ, and not only as a theological truth, *but as a position of authority from which to pray.* We're being asked to take our prayer altars to the throne room of God and there begin to pray the will of God into existence upon the earth. Paul defined this position of the church in Ephesians 1:19–23:

> I pray that you will continually experience the immeasurable greatness of God's power made available to you through faith. Then our lives will be an advertisement of this immense power as it works through you! This is the mighty power that was released when God raised Christ from the dead and exalted him to the place of highest honor and supreme authority in the heavenly realm! And now he is exalted as first above every ruler, authority, government, and realm of power in existence! He is gloriously enthroned over every name that is ever praised not only in this age, but in the age that is coming! And he alone is the leader and source of everything needed in the church. God has put everything beneath the authority of Jesus Christ and has given him the highest rank above all others. And now we, his church, are his body on the earth and that which fills him who is being filled by it!

The resurrection power of God caused Jesus to be seated far above the turmoil and change that is taking place on the earth. When we gain this perspective, we will see into the invisible realm with the eyes of faith and then begin to pray into existence what seemed impossible in the natural realm. Paul went on to tell us what the positioning of Jesus means for us in Ephesians 2:6: "He raised us up with Christ, the exalted One, and we ascended with him into the glorious perfection and authority of the heavenly realm, for we are now co-seated as one with Christ!"

We cannot pray with power, confidence, and authority if our line-of-sight is only what we see taking place around us. Our prayers must be created and released from the perspective of heaven. It's from our position in Christ, seated at the right hand of God, that we gain a perspective of prayer that is infused with a boldness that comes from seeing this life from God's perspective. Jesus said that He only did what He saw the Father doing. The same applies to us. To pray the will of God means that I must first understand His will.

PLEADING WITH GOD ON THE SEA OF GLASS

There are times of desperation when we must bring our holy pleadings for others before the throne of grace—the throne of the Righteous Judge—and to Jesus, the mediator of a new covenant (Hebrews 12:22–24). The courtroom of heaven is open for us as intercessors, where Jesus our Advocate takes us by the arm and presents us to the Judge of all the earth!

Help me remember the past. Let's debate! (Isaiah 43:26)

Come now, and let's deliberate the next steps together. (Isaiah 1:18; Job 23:3–7)

Presenting your case and laying out your arguments pleases God. He invites us to come. We were never meant to pray meaningless words. Take the Word of God and put God in remembrance of what's written. This will cause you to be moved with compassion as you engage your heart in true intercession. Your determination will be strengthened as you come into His presence with your just cause. Those who prevail with God are those who are not afraid to deliberate with Him for the next steps. Faith wrestles with God until He blesses us. These "holy wrestling matches" are the expressions of a burning heart in love with His name.

This holy debate becomes a passionate presentation of the many reasons why God should answer our plea. We never plead as an adversary; instead, we plead as His friend. Petition the court of heaven for an injunction against satan to end his harassment. The Advocate with the Father will give you the words. Praying the Scriptures is basic for every intercessor. When you pray the prayers of the Bible with a throne room perspective, you are praying a perfect prayer. We are not pleading for our will; we're praying for God's will. And His will is revealed in what He has written.

Your Father in heaven has invited you into the throne zone. You can come and bring your requests and pleadings before His throne of grace. He will answer you, His chosen one, out of His heart of wisdom and love for you.

What Does Prayer from the Throne of God Look Like?

- **It is prayer in the resurrection authority of Christ:** "I pray that you will continually experience the immeasurable greatness of God's power made available to you through faith. Then our lives will be an advertisement of this immense power as it works through you! This is the same mighty power that raised Christ from the dead" (Ephesians 1:19–20). Death tried to hold Jesus back, but the prison door of death was kicked in by the power of Christ's resurrection. When you see death trying to raise its false authority over your situation, run to your position in Christ and declare your victory in prayer from the throne of God. As that kind of prayer is released, the kingdoms of earth will be shaken with resurrection power.

- **It is the kind of prayer that feels the touch of the Father's hand.** You and I are also at the Father's right hand because we are now joined to Christ. Christ is seated at the right hand of the Father, and you and I are there together in Christ, in that position to experience an intimacy with God that will drive the release of the prayer of faith. Prayers of faith are birthed from people who know and experience intimacy with God. You're not distant from Him! Never! Pray with confidence as one who is forever united with your Redeemer.

- **It is prayer that is birthed in a place far above the turmoil.** The social, political, and economic strains taking place on the earth do not affect this kind of prayer. Prayer from above is not affected by the conditions down below. As you pray from the throne of God, you are praying as a child of God. To a religious spirit, you will appear headstrong, maybe even precocious. Don't worry about how other people feel. You are a child of God who has access to the Father 24/7. We are positioned with the one who is far above it all: "And now he is exalted as first above every ruler, authority, government, and realm of power in existence!" (Ephesians 1:21). That should breed confidence in you!

- **This kind of prayer flows from the revelation of the headship of Jesus Christ:** "He alone is the leader and source of everything needed in the church. God has put everything beneath the authority of Jesus Christ and has given him the highest rank above all others" (Ephesians

1:22). Praying from the throne of God towards earth will speak to areas in the world system that are living independent of God. Headship brings order. Prayer from the throne of God will declare headship over the disorder and rebellion that is robbing the earth of God's joy. Rebellion will be subdued, wars will be averted, and national leaders will yield to the word of the Lord when the church prays.

There are social and political transitions taking place right now that will someday be traced back to prayers from someone praying from their position in Christ, at the right hand of the Father. These prayers will not struggle in human effort in an attempt to convince God to move, but rather they will flow down with the anointing of heaven that will set in motion supernatural change. Authority flows down from the head, and so should the prayers of His saints. Strongholds that many Christians have thought were too far gone for change will suddenly change. *God is about to change what appears to be unchangeable. And your prayers are going to make the difference!*

Pray this today: God, I see there is nothing you cannot do! You have brought me into your throne room to pray to you this day. I honor you and take my place as your willing intercessor. Give me the prayer assignments you want to give me this day. I want to change the world through my prayers. Amen.

24

Ezekiel's Vision, the Fiery Cherubim

In my thirtieth year ... I looked, and I saw a
windstorm coming out of the north—an immense cloud with
flashing lightning and surrounded by brilliant light. The center
of the fire looked like glowing metal, and in the fire was what
looked like four living creatures. In appearance their form was
human, but each of them had four faces and four wings ... Fire
moved back and forth among the creatures; it was bright, and
lightning flashed out of it. The creatures sped back and forth like
flashes of lightning.
As I looked at the living creatures, I saw a wheel on the
ground beside each creature with its four faces. This was the
appearance and structure of the wheels: They sparkled like topaz,
and all four looked alike. Each appeared to be made like a wheel
intersecting a wheel. As they moved, they would go in any one of
the four directions the creatures faced ... When the living creatures
moved, the wheels beside them moved; and when the living

creatures rose from the ground, the wheels also rose. … Spread out
above the heads of the living creatures was what looked something
like a vault, sparkling like crystal, and awesome.
Above the vault over their heads was what looked like
a throne of lapis lazuli, and high above on the throne was a
figure like that of a man. I saw that from what appeared to be
his waist up he looked like glowing metal, as if full of fire, and
that from there down he looked like fire; and brilliant light
surrounded him. Like the appearance of a rainbow in the clouds
on a rainy day, so was the radiance around him. This was the
appearance of the likeness of the glory of the LORD. *When I saw*
it, I fell facedown.

EZEKIEL 1:1, 4–6, 13–17, 19, 22, 26–28 NIV

Ezekiel was a visionary prophet. He saw the heavens open up like Jacob, Nathaniel, and John did. "In his thirtieth year the heavens were opened and he saw visions of God" (Ezekiel 1:1). Ezekiel was both a prophet and a priest (1:2). And every priest who joined the temple priesthood was required to wait until he was thirty years old before they were inducted into the priesthood (Numbers 4:3). This was to be the year Ezekiel was to begin his ministry as a priest, but he and his people were in exile! There was no temple, and therefore no ministry to perform. Ezekiel was denied the opportunity that every priest dreamed about: coming before the Lord and into the temple to worship Him. But God had other plans for this priest. He was going to anoint him as a prophet instead.

Ezekiel began his prophetic ministry as a watchman at the age of thirty (Ezekiel 3:17). He had been separated to be a priest, but he also became the anointed prophet to Israel. And as an enthroned intercessor, Ezekiel had a throne-room encounter by the River

Kebar. *Kebar* means "long ago." It was the river of long ago, the river of revelation knowledge that God has kept from eternity.

The divine hand of the Lord came upon Ezekiel and anointed him as a prophet. Immediately, he was taken into the Spirit realm and saw an immense windstorm: a whirlwind of divine activity, a hurricane of holiness, a tempest of truth. What a vision this was! It was glowing, and there was flashing and a twisting pillar of cloud and fire. How would one come into that whirlwind and survive? It was wind, fire, and a spiritual volcano. Before Ezekiel's eyes, he saw the spinning fire of glory! And as he gazed upon this pillar of fire, he saw four living creatures walking in the fire, just like Nebuchadnezzar had seen four "men" in a different fire (Daniel 3:25). These living creatures all appeared in their form as men too (Ezekiel 1:5). The living creatures that Ezekiel saw were like men—intercessors in the fire!

Scholars conclude that Ezekiel's living creatures were, in fact, cherubim. They become a spiritual picture of the man who stands before God, the Lord Jesus Christ. With a face on each side, each one represents Jesus as seen in the four different Gospels. There was a face of a man, a lion, an ox, and an eagle, each representing the four-fold nature of the man Christ Jesus. Yet they also represent the ministry of Jesus before the throne: Jesus, our magnificent intercessor. As one with Him, the enthroned intercessors are to join in partnership with Him and become the fiery "cherubim" with wings touching one another, flying in perfect unity! Intercessors, it's time for us to touch wings! As you link arms (or wings) with others and network together with the prayer partners of Jesus, the glory storm will come over our land.

What about the wheels? And what is "the spirit of the living creatures that was in the wheels?" I believe these spinning wheels speak of three things:

1. The spinning wheels of God are generators of power. The wheels spin as the saints pray on earth. The more prayer, the more power is released. It's the prayers of the saints that cause the wheels to spin.

2. These wheels within wheels are like heavenly gyroscopes of glory that turn as we intercede! Our place is before the Father, showing our faces to Him and crying out for the whirlwind of divine activity to stir the hearts of men to worship and surrender to God.

3. The wheels also speak of government. God's kingdom is in motion as it comes to the earth. The throne of God sits on wheels (Daniel 7:9). The governmental throne of the universe sits on spinning wheels of glory! And God, the Father, governs on top of these wheels.

When you look at the earth's rotation around the sun, you'll see an example of a spinning wheel within a spinning wheel. As the earth spins, it rotates around the spinning sun. This is how God created His universe to operate. It all spins around His throne as His redeemed ones, His living creatures, pray on the crystal pavement.

And a wheel does not move by itself. It must be pushed, pulled, or driven. There must be a power or force that causes the wheels to spin. Ezekiel's vision was of the "spirit of the living creatures" which caused the wheels to turn. It was as though the living creatures themselves were the ones exerting the power to cause the wheels to roll. They moved the wheels by spirit-power.

> When the creatures moved, they [the wheels] also moved; when the creatures stood still, they also stood still; and when the creatures rose from the ground, the wheels rose along with them, because the spirit of the living creatures was in the wheels. (Ezekiel 1:21 NIV)

The government of God (His throne set on wheels) moves as the living creatures (intercessors) flow as one in the power of the Spirit of God within them. As they rise up in intercession, the wheels of God also rise up along with them. The partnership of heaven and earth begins to happen.

The wheels had rainbow rims and were high, with wheels within wheels. Spread out over the heads of the creatures was an expanse of pavement like sapphire, sparkling like ice. Think about that for a moment. You stand upon the sapphire pavement when you offer your prayers to Him! It's like a great Sea of Glass mingled with fire, a sparkling sapphire pavement clear as crystal with fire flashing upon it (Revelation 4:6; 15:2). You could hear the rushing wings of the cherubim! They were so powerful that they sounded like an army and like the voice of the Lord. They stirred up the winds as they rode the wheels. This is a picture of God's end-time intercessors, of you and me as we cry out for God's power to move.

> The appearance of the living creatures was like burning coals of fire or like torches. Fire moved back and forth among the creatures; it was bright, and lightning flashed out of it. The creatures sped back and forth like flashes of lightning. (Ezekiel 1:13–14 NIV)

The Lord's living ones are like lightning flashing. They're executing orders from their commanding officer. Like John the

Baptist, you can become a burning and shining torch. Let the lightning of God flash within you!

Take another look at what Ezekiel saw: a whirlwind, a rainbow of glory, the jasper throne, the sapphire pavement, cherubim, the mushroom cloud of His presence, flashing lightning, spirit beings beneath the throne surrounded by brilliant light, the center of the fire looking like glowing metal, the amber glow of the radiance of God, and sparkling wheels. Does this make prayer a little more exciting for you? How can you be bored in a prayer meeting when you see yourself before this heavenly whirlwind? How can you not help but to be overwhelmed! Remember that this is the scene every time you come to prayer before God. What an adventure!

The rainbow of promise encircles you as you stand before the throne. And if you look closely, you'll see that every saint has a crown of gold on his head! As we stand before the throne as intercessors, we have golden crowns upon our heads. What an honor God has bestowed on us! Can you picture it? There's an energy unleashed by your prayers with powerful answers released from the throne. Every time we lift our hearts toward God in prayer, an angel takes the incense in his hand, mixes it with fire from the altar of heaven, and flings it back to the earth. And as this fire enters the atmosphere of earth, it creates a shock wave of power that becomes spiritual thunder. This should give us encouragement to pray!

Around the throne, the angels are crying out, "Holy!" And the more of Him they see, the more they cry out. After all, what would you say if you saw His glory? God invites each one of us to pass through the mushroom cloud of holy smoke, walk on the sapphire pavement, past the spinning sparkling wheels, past the rainbow, the flashes of lightning, the peals of thunder, and participate in the purposes of God. We are His kingdom officials who come to ask for divine intervention! Your intercession is urgent kingdom business. He's the King of Kings, and we are His royal priesthood (Revelation 1:6, 5:10). We intercede to one who reigns over kings. This should help those who have an identity crisis. This King invites us to His throne and washes us in His love. We are enthroned with Him as kings to intercede! Genesis 2 says that God made man lord over the earth and gave man the power to take dominion and exercise authority over every living thing.

Jesus wants to be the "Amen" to your prayers (Revelation 3:1). Join Him as one of His enthroned intercessors. We were made to breathe together with Him. You will influence destiny every time you pray. Approach Him with faith, courage, boldness, and by the power of the blood. Wisdom, grace, and strategies are released at the throne room because the answers we need are not on earth; they're in heaven. His wheels spin in response to our prayers. This is so powerful!

By contrast, we have already come near to God in a totally different realm, the Zion-realm, for we have entered the city of the Living God which is the New Jerusalem in heaven! We have joined the festal gathering of myriads of angels in their joyous celebration! And as members of the church of the Firstborn all our names have been legally registered as citizens of heaven! And we have come before God who judges all, and who lives among the spirits of the righteous who have been made perfect in his eyes! And we have come to Jesus who established a new covenant with his blood sprinkled upon the mercy seat; blood that continues to speak from heaven, "forgiveness," a better message than Abel's blood that cries from the earth, "justice." (Hebrews 12:22–24)

Pray this today: Father God, I draw near to you today in the heavenly realm. I take my place next to Jesus, my Prayer Partner. I bring before you my heart with all its needs. I want you to use me as I pray to you today. Give me inside information, prophetic revelation that I can use in my ministry of prayer. I pour out my heart before you this day, my King, and my God. Amen.

25

PRAYER PARTNERS WITH JESUS

The heavens belong to our God, they are his alone,
but he has given us the earth and put us in charge.

PSALM 115:16

Promotion is coming to the body of Christ. Our Lord Jesus is preparing His bride for reigning with Him. He wants to include us in the governmental affairs of His universe. As we labor alongside the Son of God in prayer, we become His "helpmates" in fulfilling the Father's will for planet Earth. It's a great mystery: Jesus wants us to share His throne!

God has given the dominion of the earth to mankind. In the beginning, Adam and Eve were entrusted with the affairs of earth and were created to be God's agents, governors of the planet. But this right to rule was forfeited when mankind fell into the darkness of selfish pride and independence. When Jesus came, He restored our right to rule and reign with Him. And He's raising up men and women to rule with Him. When you're praying, don't ever forget you're really touching heaven and changing the earth.

The devil only has the power to do on earth what the church allows and yields to him. As governors of this planet, the church is to exercise the authority of the kingdom of God in all things. Out of intimacy with God in prayer, we're able to destroy the works of darkness and release the deeds of light and glory to the earth.

As His covenant partners and co-heirs, we have His life in us; we're sharers of one common life. We must become so conformed to His image that our deeds multiply and amplify His very works. And the goal of our lives must be more than having a ministry … we must be able to say, "My true life is the Anointed One, and dying means gaining more of him" (Philippians 1:21). Remember this: God loves His Son so much, He is determined to fill heaven and earth with people just like Him.

You're not just a human being on your way to heaven. You're a duplicate of the Son of God having an earthly experience! And your life is O.J.T. (on-the-job-training) because you'll be ruling over the universe one day. You're in schooling for ruling and training for reigning! Earth's workshop will finish your preparation to sit on the throne with Jesus Christ, ruling over angels and nations forever! Living prayer, walking prayer, night and day prayer is coming to a church near you!

Come on, intercessor: you must be diligent to become that prayer partner Jesus is looking for. May His eyes gaze upon you and find your heart to be a manger, a place that gives birth to eternal purpose. With His cross as your torch of truth and seated in the throne room, you take the kingdom by force. You're the one who knows firsthand the miracle power of God.

THE SPIRIT OF PRAYER

The Holy Spirit has come to teach us to pray. Whenever you yield to Him, or make room for Him and obey Him even a little, He leads you to prayer. The life within you is a life of prayer. He knows what to pray and waits to be your personal prayer mentor. The Holy Spirit is interceding and partnering with us as we pray in Him (Romans 8:26–27).

As you have fellowship with God, the Holy Spirit flows through you, and the Spirit of prayer fills you. For whenever we live in the spirit, prayer rises from within. We move with God, and God moves with us. And heaven's heart is fulfilled when it's flowing through you. The prayers that move heaven are not released until they come from you.

Elijah prayed through the spirit of prayer. Even though he was a man with similar problems and passions as any other, he prayed, and the heavens closed. He prayed again, and the heavens opened. Elijah cooperated and flowed with the spirit of prayer. "He prayed and received supernatural answers" (James 5:17)—what this literally says is that Elijah *prayed with prayer* or *prayed in prayer*. As he prayed, true prayer in the Spirit came forth. He prayed, but the Spirit prayed through him. Elijah became a prayer partner with the Spirit within him. They breathed together the same request. This type of prayer in prayer must come in order for the church to move into the season of the open heavens.

As we pray, our spirit and the Holy Spirit join as one and enter heaven with a request that will be answered. This type of prayer expresses God Himself, not just His will. God's very life comes flowing through us as we pray to the Father. When He prays, you pray with Him. When you pray, God prays with you. He is one with you inside and out! In this prayer moment, you and God cannot be separated, for you are mingled as one.

As friends of God, we should be able to complete one another's sentences. We know each other that well! Let Him whisper His thoughts into you as you pray. This is what both Paul and Jude call "praying in the Holy Spirit" (Ephesians 5:18; Jude 20). Both the spirit of the intercessor and the Spirit of God cry to the Father for an answer. This God-Man prayer combo is what the universe has waited for. "And now we, his church, are his body on the earth and that which fills him who is being filled by it!" (Ephesians 1:23). Man must become the container of God and join eternity in the divine symphony of prayer on the Sea of Glass before the throne.

ALMIGHTY & SONS, INC.

Your Father has included you in His construction company. He's the senior partner, but since you are His child, He has included you as a co-signer to all the legal work required in running the business (ruling over the nations). As a helpmate of Jesus Christ, God's plan is to partner with you. There are certain things we must do as part of this partnership of "Almighty & Sons." There are some things God will not do for us.

We must be the ones to pray, to fast, to give generously, to evangelize, to study the Word of God, to love our spouses and children, to go to the unreached tribes, to serve our local church, and to develop a rich devotional life in God. All of these things are awaiting our activity, our doing. It is not God's job to do these things for us. These are the secrets and mysteries of God.

Paul was one who devoted himself to the grace of God. He understood that it was God plus nothing. Yet he refused to let grace be wasted on an undisciplined life. He labored in the grace of God. He worked in the energy of grace to become a follower of the Lamb in all things. But when it was all said and done, he knew it was only by the grace of God that he accomplished anything. Listen to his heart: "But God's amazing grace has made me who I am! And his grace to me was not fruitless. In fact, I worked harder than all the rest, yet not in my own strength but God's, for his empowering grace is poured out upon me" (1 Corinthians 15:10). Grace works hard. Grace gives us strength to finish. Grace gives us the power to partner with divine energy. God will continually revitalize you, implanting within you the passion to do what pleases Him ... but we still have to work out our practical salvation day by day (Philippians 2:12–13).

THE DIVINE PARTNERSHIP

God has chosen to adapt His intentions and deeds through this interaction with us called prayer. Prayer moves God. The all-powerful God is stirred to action by our prayers. He knows all things, but He will withhold certain miracles and activities until we pray and seek Him. God told Moses that He had seen and heard and felt the affliction of the Hebrew slaves in Egypt, but He waited and waited until their cries burdened Him and He could not hold back any longer (Judges 10:16). Intercession activates heaven. It's the on-ramp for the heavenly super highway of miracles. Prayer releases power to the earth. What a mystery!

According to Genesis 2, God created man with a will and the ability to decide and determine his future. God has a will and man has a will. Whenever man's will is not in agreement with God's will, God is limited. Man's will affects God's plan and purposes. The church of Jesus Christ can extend God's kingdom or delay the coming of that kingdom.

When the church places its will under God, He will move on earth the same way He will move in eternity. If we don't oppose God here, then heaven's will is done on earth. When the church decides, God acts. The Lord wants a bridal partner who will work with Him as a co-laborer with God (2 Corinthians 6:1).

When Israel wandered in the wilderness of the pre-promised land, God was faithful to supply them with all their needs, including food and water for nearly one million people. This was an amazing miracle that continually reminded His people that God was one with them. Listen to one of the miracles God accomplished in providing water: "The Lord said to Moses, 'Gather the people together and I will give them water.' Then Israel sang this song; 'Spring up, O well! Sing about it, about the well that the princes dug, that the nobles of the people sank—the nobles with scepters and staffs'" (Numbers 21:16–18 NIV).

The Lord brought them to the place of water, but they had to dig the well! So it is with the divine partnership. The Lord requires our participation. He longs for a partner that will discover the treasures of His purpose and then move out in active fulfillment to achieve it. The "princes" and the "nobles" are the partners who have grasped this principle and set themselves to perform it.

Are you a noble ditch digger? Will you be a partner with heaven, or will you be one who waits and waits for something God calls you to perform? Without any labor, God cannot bless. But when we know the purposes of God and sing (prophesy) to our well from the throne room, we step into divine partnership, we touch the place of miracles (i.e., the supernatural flow of water). Use your scepter of authority and the staff (rod) of power in your hand and bring it to pass, O mighty ones who do His bidding!

SOWING AND REAPING IN PRAYER

The incredible principle of sowing and reaping applies to prayer in ways many do not comprehend. This is not only a principle for finances; it is also a foundational principle for the spirit-energized life. In Isaiah 61:11, God promises that righteousness (*deliverance* in The Passion Translation) will blossom before all the nations. This is a prophetic promise of the glorious church arising in holy partnership with her Bridegroom-King. This prophetic word must come to pass. God's purposes will surely blossom and come forth just as the spring brings new growth in the gardens of the earth. But something has to be sown first—something must first be planted if it's to spring forth! Only what's been planted in the earth will bud to new life ... there has to be a human partnership with God in planting seeds of righteousness and praise if they are to spring up and bring light to the nations. God needs His children to plant the right seeds so that the earth brings forth the right fruit. We have to sow righteousness and praise before the nations if we are to reap of the same kind!

Listen: The future state of a glorious church releasing light and power to the nations depends upon watchmen on earth who will never be silent and who will give God no rest until He makes His promise a living thing. This is ordained prayer. This is sowing prayer that will reap a harvest of righteousness. Where there is no one to partner with God in prayer, righteousness is not found, and the nations perish. There must be a high level of cooperation with the intent of God and the activity of the church to accomplish the cosmic goals we seek. This exhilarating prayer will not grow silent until the light of glory shines upon us!

We work together with God to determine the affairs of men—and even future events. If we learn to pray with Jesus, breathing out His prayers on the earth, we can shape history. Think of Joshua commanding the sun to stand still ... God needed his prayer to work that miracle.

In a way, in everything God wants to do on earth, He wants man to work with Him from the throne room to bring it to pass. We become the voice of the Lord and the scepter of righteousness in His hand. The High Priests of the Old Testament entered the Holy Place alone ... but our Great High Priest invites us to come and be partners with Him in the Holy of Holies.

The Father has given His Son to be the head over the church. He is the head, and we are the body (1 Corinthians 12:27). Yet, the head cannot say to the rest of the body, "I don't need you" (1 Corinthians 12:21). Jesus needs His body to fulfill the plans of the Father. All of the destiny of the universe is waiting for the head and the body to flow as one until we fully express the nature of the Father. Then Jesus will have a place to "lay His head" (Luke 9:58).

SHAPERS OF THE FUTURE

Prayer is the power that shapes the future, moving God to fulfill what is promised and stirring earth to respond to heaven. The future belongs to the intercessors. They're the ones who exercise spiritual defiance over what is seen and insist on a new inevitability in the affairs of earth. With the politics of hope, intercessors are filled with a vision of what can be if they pray.

God will intervene in all the affairs of earth if intercessors will pray. And the prayer of agreement will release the dreamed-of future, creating the reality that is hoped for. Will you be a shaper of the future? Will you enter the throne room and lock arms with Jesus and partner with Him?

God longs for an earth-being to agree with Him. As we take

our place in the throne room, the true purpose of creation falls into place. God has a representative and partner on earth that will exercise dominion over what needs to be changed. He allows us to take part in the councils of eternity. It's our supreme task to enter into this alliance with the throne room, calling out, "Thy kingdom come, thy will be done. On earth, like it is in the throne room on the Sea of Glass."

The Lord longs for a partner to join Him in prayer. Our prayers not only meet the needs of man, but they meet the needs of God. By uniting our hearts in the prayer of agreement (earth and heaven together), God's desired future is released from the throne.

Prayer is the Father's gateway to have His will escorted to the earth. This is why He implores us to ask, search, and knock. These imperative commands must be fulfilled if God is to fully implement divine strategies in a fallen world. We have been commanded to command. We have been required to insist for intervention, to be asking for the sick, the poor, the lost, and the weak. Prayer is, in a sense, ordering God to bring His kingdom near. It's using our authority to conform the present into the desirable future. It's time to use our kingdom power to flood the earth with His purposes and plans.

Our prayers wake Him up (so to speak) and stir Him to action. They set God free to act on our behalf. It's sending a letter to heaven's celestial capital where it's sorted, read, and responded to. Our words are powerful. They have power as a co-creator with God to shape the future together with him as His partners. God says to the church, *My realm created your realm, but your realm moves my realm through prayer. Move me to move the world, and I will bring my kingdom to you. I'm about to "tag" you and you're "it."*

What if you were gripped with this reality? Would you want to pray more for His kingdom to come to the devastated places on earth? Far from being passive, prayer becomes a means of creating action where there is nothing but darkness. Our prayer-voice becomes a trumpet that heralds what God is about to do. Perhaps we are those angels that hurl coals of fire from off the altar to the earth by means of fervent prayer (Revelation 8).

The yoke of Jesus (Matthew 11:28–30) is a yoke of union, not toilsome labor. It is the blending of the human and the divine. This is what took place in the manger. The God-Man was born as a prototype for a coming people. Our Lord Jesus took this yoke when He was born a man. Now Jesus extends a yoke to His church, a yoke of union with Him. It is a yoke of divine partnering in the affairs of heaven.

Earth is invited to rule with heaven in a holy oneness. This is where God wants us to go as we approach the wedding feast of the Lamb and His wife. It is a cooperative prayer initiative. You and God in a holy "co-op." It's the purpose of God to make you into a "look-alike" of Jesus Christ, reflecting His image, flowing in His power, praying His prayers.

The day will come when you will be able to say, like David said, "I am prayer" (Psalm 109:4). Yes, the Hebrew text actually says, "I am prayer!" God will have a people who have become prayer. You cannot separate the person from the prayer. To pray as His partner will one day make you prayer itself! Beloved, it's time to become a prayer partner with Jesus!

Pray this today: Father God, give me a greater love for my brothers and sisters. May our fellowship together in prayer always be sweet and life-giving. Help me to bond easily to other believers. I lay aside my preferences to put others above myself. Let me walk with others the same way you walked with your disciples—demonstrating love and mercy each day. Amen.

Suggested Reading

The Power of Prayer—E. M. Bounds

Developing Your Secret Closet of Prayer—Richard Burr

The Mighty Warrior—Elizabeth Alves

Surprised by the Voice of God—Jack Deere

The Power of Prayer and Fasting—Ronnie Floyd

The Lost Art of Intercession—James Goll

Rees Howells, Intercessor—Norman Grubb

Experiencing God through Prayer—Jeanne Guyon

The Ministry of Intercession—Andrew Murray

Praying with Power—C. Peter Wagner

The Sacred Journey—Brian and Candice Simmons

The Transforming Power of Prayer—James Houston

Intercessory Prayer—Dutch Sheets

Passion for Jesus—Mike Bickle

Beyond the Veil—Alice Smith

Cross-Pollination—Lila Terhune

Invading the Privacy of God—Cecil Murphey

Kneeling on the Promises—James Goll

Seasons of Intercession—Frank DaMazio

Winning the Prayer War—Kjell Sjoberg

The Fire of Delayed Answers—Bob Sorge

Praying Hyde—E. G. Carre

Listen, God Is Speaking to You—Quin Sherrer

Acts 29 Blueprint for the House of Prayer—Terry Teykl

Three Battlegrounds—Francis Frangipane

The Hour That Changes the World—Dick Eastman

Your Kingdom Come—Michael Sullivant

Hearing God—Dallas Willard

The Watchman—Tom Hess

Wasted on Jesus—James Goll

God.com—James Alexander Langteaux

Destined for the Throne—Paul Billheimer

The Soul's Sincere Desire—Glen Clark

Moving God through Prayer—Zacharias Tanee Fomom

The Breaker Anointing—Barbara Yoder

The Powers That Be—Walter Wink

Governmental Prayer—Noel Woodroffe

Incense and Thunder—Dudley Hall

Teach Me to Pray—Andrew Murray

ABOUT THE AUTHORS

Dr. Brian Simmons is known as a passionate lover of God and the lead translator of The Passion Translation, a new heart-level Bible translation that conveys God's passion for people and His world by translating the original, life-changing message of God's Word for modern readers. Brian and his wife, Candice, travel full-time as speakers and Bible teachers.

For more information on Passion and Fire Ministries and a complete listing of their teaching materials, contact:

Passion & Fire Ministries
PO Box 4068
Madison, CT
06443
U.S.A.
passionandfire.com
passionmovement.com
877–566–4289